The
Property Investment
Playbook

Also by the authors

Property Investment for Beginners
Robert Heaton

Essential Property Investment Calculations
Robert Heaton

The Property Investment Playbook – Volume 1
Robert Heaton & Ye Feng

The Property Investment Playbook – Volume 2
Robert Heaton & Ye Feng

The Property Investment Playbook

Volume 2

A complete course in property investment,
buy-to-let investing and property development

Robert Heaton & Ye Feng

Get the free resources

I've prepared some free materials to accompany the book. All you need to do to access them is head over to my website. These materials include the following:

- a spreadsheet for assessing HMO property deals
- a list of all the property auction houses in the UK
- a list of all REITs listed on the London Stock Exchange
- a list of SIPPs that permit commercial property

The spreadsheets are the ones I use personally in my own property investments. It's all completely free with no sell on. Just sign up at my website at:

www.essentialproperty.net/playbook-vol-2

Contents

Introduction

In 2019, the Ministry of Housing, Communities and Local Government published the results of the 2018 English Private Landlord Survey. The aim of the survey was to inform government understanding of the private rental sector. The survey revealed that almost half of landlords in England own just one rental property, and the average number of properties owned was just three. On the one hand, these results might not be too surprising – after all, it takes time and money to invest in property, and many investors and landlords are happy to operate on a small scale, using rental profits to subsidise their incomes and their pensions. However, on the other hand, these results also tell us that only a few landlords and investors actually succeed in growing large portfolios, say with five or more properties, and those that do are definitely in the minority – a result that's more surprising through the lens that it's easier to grow wealth once you have some. So, what is it about this small minority of landlords and property investors that makes them so successful? What strategies do they used to fuel their success and to expand their portfolios in a way most investors can only dream about, and are there advanced techniques they've mastered that others have not? That's what Volume 2 of the playbook is all about.

The Property Investment Playbook is a course designed to give an overview of all the various strategies or plays that UK property investors are using to grow their property portfolios. It's a compilation of the best and smartest techniques out there, covering everything from how to get started to more sophisticated and advanced techniques used by investors with years of experience under their belt. If you're new to property investment, the books will teach you how to get started and all of the basic strategies you'll need to succeed, including the oldies and the goodies like basic buy-to-let and light refurbishments. For experienced investors, I hope the books will challenge you to add a few new plays to your own playbook and expand your repertoire. I hope they also help you to develop a more creative mindset and come up with better and more innovative ways to do deals.

The course is split into two parts. Volume 1 is aimed at new property investors and those who've been investing for a few years, but still feel they could improve at the basics. Volume 2 is aimed at more experienced property investors, but it's also suitable for anyone looking to learn one or more of the advanced investment techniques typically reserved for experienced investors. Here's a quick overview of what's covered in Volume 2, which picks up where Volume 1 left off.

In Part Four, we'll run through all the strategies and approaches you need to know to grow your property portfolio. We'll teach you techniques that will help you make the most of the limited investment capital at your disposal and grow your portfolio faster, cover some alternative sourcing approaches, like targeting repossessed properties, buying at auction and purchasing properties off plan, that can help you to achieve below market value deals, and look at how to manage your portfolio over time, with a bit of help from the property cycle. In Part Five, we'll cover a range of advanced investment techniques that are typically only used by experienced investors. We'll look at a wide range of advanced strategies, covering everything from trading properties for a profit to HMOs. We'll also cover the more technical plays like rent-to-rent and lease options and consider some completely new investment areas, like overseas and commercial property. Each strategy we consider in Part Five of the playbook requires some level of prior knowledge, hard-won experience, or a personal network and team only possessed by well-established investors in order to be successful, but there's nothing to stop new investors from trying to get ahead of the game and studying these approaches for use later in their journey, once they have the necessary experience under their belt. We've tried to make the material as self-contained as possible, though we do refer back to the contents of Volume 1 in a small number of places, where we've deemed that material to be relevant.

All the material presented is geared towards making you a better investor by giving you an overview of the strategies and techniques you can use to take your property business and your property portfolio to the next level. In each play, we'll run through things like the keys to success and common pitfalls and mistakes to increase your chances of success, if you put this strategy into practice for yourself. If you're looking to take your strategic thinking and your investment approach to the next level and become one of a small minority of investors and landlords who manage to grow a property portfolio that's life-changing in both size and impact, my hope is this book will help you do just that.

Robert Heaton
April 2021

Basic investment terminology

In other books, you'll find all kinds of background on the different terminology and numerical underpinnings behind property investment. All of this is essential knowledge, but I'm not going to cover it again here, as there simply wouldn't be enough space. If you're looking for further background on the numbers side of property, I've written a whole book on this very topic, called *Essential Property Investment Calculations*, covering all of the calculations, numerical techniques and metrics most property investors use to assess property deals and manage their portfolios. In this book, I've tried to bring in only those details needed to understand the strategies and plays presented and how they work. That being said, there are a few key terms and fundamental metrics you need to know to read this book. Let's recap on some of these now.

Rental yield calculations

Capitalisation rate

Capitalisation rate ("cap rate" for short) is calculated as the annual net operating profit from the rental property divided by the purchase price of the property, assuming the investor buys the property without using a mortgage. Because of this, the profit calculation excludes mortgage costs:

$$Cap\ rate = \frac{Annual\ net\ operating\ profit}{Purchase\ price}$$

or

$$Cap\ rate = \frac{(Annual\ rental\ income - Annual\ rental\ costs)}{Purchase\ price}$$

We need to include all the other costs associated with running the property, i.e. marketing costs, letting agent fees, repair and maintenance costs, service charges and ground rents, etc. Capitalisation rate gives investors a measure of how good the returns are for the rental property itself, ignoring mortgage financing costs. It allows investors to compare properties on a consistent basis.

Return on investment

Return on investment ("ROI") shows us how our rental profits compare with the actual cash we have invested in the deal. ROI is the annual rental profit from the property divided by the cash you've invested in the deal. If you've bought the property in cash without a mortgage, this is the same as the cap rate, but if you've used a mortgage you'll have put in less of your own cash:

$$ROI = \frac{Annual\ rental\ profit}{Cash\ invested}$$

or

$$ROI = \frac{(Annual\ rental\ income - Annual\ rental\ costs)}{Cash\ invested}$$

When we carry out the calculation, we need to include all rental costs this time, including any mortgage costs. Equally, when we calculate the cash invested, we need to include all the cash costs of purchasing the property, like our deposit, stamp duty, valuation fees, broker costs, etc. These are all real cash costs that need to be paid upfront, so they should be included in our calculation.

ROI is our best guess at the return we're actually going to achieve on our cash. Because of this, you can even compare it with the potential returns you'd get on non-property investments, e.g. the interest we'd received on a bank account or the dividend yield on a share. It shows you how hard your money is working for you and how this compares with other available investments. For most of the plays in this book, the key number I focus on when analysing returns is the ROI. So, if you only remember one formula, this is the one to choose.

Capital growth

The calculations we've looked at above only consider the rental returns from a property. However, many property investors are also looking for capital growth. Capital growth is the uplift in the value of a property over time. It's an extra source of return for property investors, if they experience some. However, there are no guarantees you'll experience any, and the level of capital growth you can expect is inherently uncertain, as is the timeframe over which it will play out. As such, it's usually best to base your investment decisions on the two metrics we've covered above and see capital growth as more of a nice-to-have. That being said, there are plenty of investors out there who invest mainly with capital growth in mind and who try to pick an area or location where they think the prospects for future growth are strongest. The important thing to remember is that it's the market, not the investor, that controls the general level of capital growth.

Financing and leverage

Leverage is one of those words that property investors throw around all the time. Here they're talking about financial leverage, and by that we simply mean using borrowed money to invest in assets. That is, when we buy a property, we put in some of the money ourselves, and we use borrowed money from a lender or bank to purchase the rest. In short, most properties are bought using mortgages.

The two main types of mortgage you can use to invest in buy-to-let properties are repayment and interest only mortgages. With a repayment mortgage, you pay off a small amount of the loan each month plus some interest. By the end of the loan term, you'll have paid off the loan in full. With an interest only mortgage, you pay just the interest on the borrowed money each month. At the end of the loan term, you still need to pay back the original amount borrowed, so you'll need a plan for how to pay this back. With a repayment mortgage, because you pay off the loan gradually over time, your monthly repayments will be higher than with an interest only mortgage.

Payments on an interest only mortgage

It's simple to calculate the monthly repayments on an interest only mortgage. If the loan amount is A and our interest rate is i, we calculate this as follows:

$$Monthly\ payment = (A \times i)/12$$

For example, if you borrow £100,000 at a 3% p.a. interest rate, the payments will be £100,000 × 3% ÷ 12 which equals £250 per month.

Payments on a repayment mortgage

To estimate the payments on a repayment mortgage, we need a more involved formula. Here we have A as the loan amount, i as the interest rate, and T as the term (length) of the mortgage. We calculate our monthly repayments as follows:

$$Monthly\ payment = \frac{1}{12} \times \left(\frac{A \times i}{(1 - (1+i)^{-T})} \right)$$

For example, if you take out a loan of £100,000 for a term of 25 years at a 3% p.a. interest rate, the monthly payments will be as follows:

$$\frac{1}{12} \times \left(\frac{£100,000 \times 0.03}{(1 - (1.03)^{-25})} \right) = £479$$

For our technical readers, the formula above assumes (for simplicity) that your mortgage payments are paid annually in arrears – that is, all at once at the end of the year. In practice, you'll make payments on a monthly basis throughout the year, and your payments will actually be slightly less that the estimate provided by the formula above.

Interest only versus repayment

Property investors typically opt for interest only mortgages. Their thinking is that it requires lower monthly payments, so it improves their cash flow position. The investor then has a choice of whether to use the extra cash flow to pay down some of the outstanding loan balance, thereby reducing the amount they owe, or put it towards their next property purchase instead. If you're not overly comfortable with the general idea of debt, then a repayment mortgage might appear the safer choice. However, it's really a matter of personal preference and your tolerance for risk. What's more, if your plan is to grow a large portfolio, you'll likely want to opt for interest only and reinvest that extra cash flow. As such, throughout this book, we'll assume you take out interest only mortgages to finance your property investments, unless stated otherwise.

Wrapping it up

That's really all the calculations and basic terminology you need to read this book. If you're new to property investment and the short recap above wasn't enough, you can check out my book, *Essential Property Investment Calculations*, or one of the introductory property books out there for more background on the numbers side of things. With that recap out of the way, hit the lights and cue the music – it's time for the main attraction.

Part Four : Growing your property portfolio

Play # 31 – Using BRRR to recycle your cash

Early on in her property journey, Jennie had saved hard and invested in basic buy-to-let investments that needed little or no work. The returns were good, but the overall progress was slow. With her confidence and skills improving, she found herself looking for alternative approaches that could speed up her progress. One of these strategies, which she read about on a forum, combined buy-to-let investment with a refurbishment project; it offered the promise of a higher ROI and allowed the investor to "recycle" some of the cash invested, thereby leaving less money trapped in each deal. It sounded like an ideal way to maximise the returns on her hard-earned savings.

Stretching your investment capital

The biggest constraint most people face when trying to build a property portfolio is a lack of funds. There is no quick and easy fix to this problem, but there are strategies you can employ to stretch your investment capital further and speed up your progress. In this section, we'll take a look at one of the key techniques that property investors use to lower the amount of investment capital they need – known in property circles as "buy, refurbish, rent out, and refinance" or BRRR for short. We'll take a look at how this strategy works, the risks you'll face in execution and the keys to success. We'll also take a look at what type of investors this strategy is right for and the benefits it can bring, if you get it right.

How does it work?

The basic idea behind this strategy is straightforward – you buy a property, carry out a refurbishment, rent it out, and refinance it to release some (potentially all) of your original capital, lowering the amount of cash tied up in the deal.

This strategy shares a number of similarities with property flips. Firstly, the core principle at work here is that you need to "add value" to the property, so you should focus your efforts and resources on those areas that will add the most value to the final price. Secondly, you need to know your end market well and be confident that you can refinance the refurbished property at your target price. Lastly, it means you're likely to be taking on projects needing a medium or heavy refurbishment, as this is where there's more potential to add value and drive an uplift in the market value that's greater than the cost of doing the works.

Aims and objectives

In the coming pages, we're going to take a look at how this strategy works with a simple buy-to-let investment as the end goal for the project. At a high level, this play has two principal aims and objectives:

1. To lower the capital required – If you get this play right, you should be able to cut down the amount of capital tied up in the final investment.
2. To build your wealth and income faster – By "forcing equity" and leaving less money tied up, you can build your property wealth and income faster.

With this play, it's all about finding the right property to work on. You're looking for a property that needs a bit more work than most people are prepared to do, and you're using this to help you strike a better deal. At this same time, you're looking for a property you'd be prepared to buy and hold as part of your portfolio over the long term. That is, the refurbished property needs to meet all the usual investment criteria you would apply to a regular buy-to-let, including your target capitalisation rate, ROI, and its potential for capital growth.

A worked example

Let's look at a worked example, based on the figures we used in play # 20. We're going to compare the figures for a basic buy-to-let investment with what we could achieve using BRRR, if we bought a similar property in poor condition and carried out a refurbishment to bring it back up to standard. Let's take a closer look at the figures involved.

The basic buy-to-let investment

Our basic buy-to-let investment, Property A, was a two-bedroom, two-bathroom apartment 10 to 15 minutes' walk from Leeds City Centre. The key assumptions were as follows: (a) we could secure the property for £160,000 with negotiation; (b) to finance the deal, we would use a 75% loan-to-value interest only mortgage at a 3% p.a. interest rate; (c) the flat needs no refurbishment, but we would let the property out furnished, with the cost of furnishings being around £2,000; (d) the property would generate £208 of profit per month or around £2,496 per year before tax. Our total cash tied up in the deal, after allowing for the additional cost of stamp duty, legal expenses and other purchase costs, was £50,000.

The equivalent BRRR investment

Suppose that instead of buying a basic buy-to-let investment that's ready-to-go, we can buy an almost identical property that's in need of a refurbishment. This is our equivalent BRRR buy-to-let property, and we'll call it Property B. We're going to assume that because the property needs a lot of work, we can secure it for a knock-down price of £110,000 and then spend time, money and effort bringing it back up to standard, thereby reinstating its "true" market value of £160,000. Our key assumptions are as follows: (a) we purchase the property using a 70% loan-to-value bridging loan; (b) the building works will cost around £20,000, including a 10% contingency fund; (c) we incur financing costs of £8,430 in relation to the bridging finance, with an estimated time of six months to complete the works and an additional two months to complete the refinancing.

	Property A	Property B
Property purchase price	£160,000	£110,000

Deal financing

	Property A	Property B
Financing method	Mortgage	Bridging
Loan-to-value	75%	70%
Loan amount	£120,000	£77,000
Deposit	£40,000	£33,000

Cash invested

	Property A	Property B
Deposit	£40,000	£33,000
Stamp duty	£5,500	£3,300
Furnishing costs	£2,000	£2,000
Building works (with 10% contingency)	-	£20,000
Financing costs (see later for breakdown)	-	£8,430
Fees (e.g. valuation, survey, legal advice)	£2,500	£2,500
Total cash invested	£50,000	£69,230

The figures in the table above set out the total cash invested for both deals. For Property A, our basic buy-to-let investment, this is £50,000, including the deposit plus additional costs like stamp duty, furnishings and fees related to the property purchase, e.g. valuation, survey and legal costs. For Property B, our equivalent BRRR investment, we've invested cash totalling £69,230 at the point immediately before we refinance. This includes the cost of the deposit, stamp duty, furnishings and fees related to the property purchase, but it also includes the additional cost of the building works and bridging finance.

Here comes the magic

At this point, we've invested more cash in the equivalent BRRR deal than the basic buy-to-let, but all that is about to change. With the refurbishment work complete, we're now going to refinance the property using a traditional mortgage product. For this, we're going to assume we can refinance using an equivalent mortgage to that used in our Property A example – that is, we will use a 75% loan-to-value interest only mortgage at a 3% p.a. interest rate. When we do so, we will borrow 75% of the *uplifted* property value of £160,000, rather than the £110,000 we paid for the property. That's what we (and hopefully the mortgage provider) believe the property is worth. So, we'll borrow £120,000 (75% × £160,000) and we'll use this to pay off the outstanding bridging loan of £77,000. Let's take a look at how this affects the amount of cash we have tied up in the deal.

Total cash invested before refinancing	£69,230
Less: Money received from new loan (75% × £160,000)	(£120,000)
Plus: Repayment of bridging loan (70% ×£110,000)	£77,000
Total cash invested after refinancing	£26,230

We originally invested £69,230 in the BRRR deal, but the refinancing has allowed us to take £43,000 out of the deal (the difference between the new borrowing of £120,000 and the outstanding bridging loan of £77,000). That means we've now got just £26,230 of cash tied up in the deal, compared with £50,000 for Property A for the basic buy-to-let investment.

The impact on ROI and net worth

Finally, let's take a look at the overall impact of this strategy on the ROI achieved and on our net worth. The final profit and cash flow achieved is the same for both Property A and Property B; that is, both will generate an annual pre-tax profit of £2,496. However, the ROI achieved with the BRRR strategy is much higher, owing to the smaller amount of cash needed. The basic buy-to-let investment generates an ROI of 5.0% p.a. (£2,496 ÷ £50,000 cash invested) before tax; the equivalent BRRR investment generates a pre-tax ROI of 9.5% p.a. (£2,496 ÷ £26,230). That's almost double the ROI and this makes sense – the investments generate the *same profit*, but the BRRR deal leaves us with *less cash invested* in the deal.

The BRRR strategy is also a more effective wealth-building tool. Let's take a look at why. With the basic buy-to-let investment, we've acquired assets worth £42,000 through the purchase of Property A – we own £40,000 of equity in the property (the market value of £160,000 less the outstanding loan of £120,000) as well as furnishings with £2,000. We've acquired these assets for a total cash investment of £50,000. However, with the equivalent BRRR investment, we have acquired the same assets worth £42,000 for a cash investment of £26,230. In short, we've spent £23,770 less (£50,000 less £26,230) with the BRRR strategy to acquire the same assets. We've done this by driving a hard bargain during the initial purchase and by using a refurbishment to add value.

A word on bridging finance

In general, it's not appropriate to use a mortgage to finance the initial purchase of the property using the BRRR strategy. That's because mortgages are a longer-term financing product that's intended to be held for a number of years. So, even if you are able to find a mortgage product that doesn't have any specific penalties for early repayment, lenders don't like it if you refinance too soon after the initial purchase. If you are planning to refinance quickly after your refurb is complete, that means you'll need to use bridging finance instead.

We discussed bridging loans in play # 25 of Volume 1. To recap, bridging loans up to 70% loan-to-value are typically available for this kind of project. The fees you pay tend to vary quite a bit between lenders. In the worked example above, I've estimated the financing costs associated with the bridging loan as the sum of the following:

- an initial valuation fee, e.g. £500 in this example
- an arrangement fee of 1%-2% of the loan, e.g. 1% × £77,000 = £770
- the interest costs, e.g. 1% per month × 8 months × £77,000 = £6,160
- the lender's legal fees, e.g. assumed to be £1,000 here

In this example, the fees and charges come to £8,430, but in practice there could be other charges on top. Some lenders will add exit-fees, which might be say 1% of the amount borrowed. Also, if you arrange the loan through a broker, their fee could be up to 1% of the loan amount. So, it isn't cheap, but it can give you access to deals and projects that you don't have the cash savings for yourself. Just make sure these costs are fully factored into your calculations.

Lastly, it's worth saying that if you're prepared to wait for a number of years before you carry out the refinancing step and live with having a larger amount of cash tied up in the deal over this period, you could consider using a traditional mortgage instead. In this case, you should opt for a short, fixed rate mortgage of say two years and look to refinance at the end of this period.

What kind of results are possible?

Now that we understand how this play works and we've looked at an example, it's worth discussing what kinds of results are possible with this approach.

BRRR opportunities are easiest to find and the results are at their best where activity in a local market is slightly depressed. When there are fewer buyers but ample sellers and when there's a lack of competition for these types of projects, you're more likely to be able to secure the property for a lower price. That will give you the best chance of securing the margin you need to recycle part or all of your cash. You do, however, need to be confident that you can remortgage the refurbished property at your target price, so there needs to be sufficient activity to be able to point to those recent sales and comparables.

In general, you want to be hunting for these types of deals in areas that haven't yet become the next property hotspot. An area that's on-the-up and at the early stages of a turnaround is ideal. You can use the fact the area is becoming more fashionable to your advantage and to lower your downside risk. That is, given the choice between an area where prices in general are increasing and one where they're decreasing, you should pick the former. At the very least, you should pick an area where you expect local prices will remain stable over the time frame of the refurbishment. The fact you're going to rent the property out rather than sell it on also means you'll want the property to meet your regular investment criteria as far as ROI, yield and capital growth prospects are concerned.

If you do everything right and you don't have any hiccups, you should be able to achieve good results with this approach. But what does good look like? For me, good means the following: (a) being able to pull out half or more of the cash I've invested in the deal after the refinancing; (b) securing a decent uplift in the final ROI versus a basic buy-to-let investment that's ready to go. Both these elements need to be present in a BRRR deal to justify the time and effort that goes into a project like this. It's sometimes possible to achieve even better results than this, and there are stories of experienced investors being able to pull out all of the cash they've invested and achieving an infinite ROI. In my experience, these deals are rare in practice, but they do make for good headlines.

Common pitfalls and mistakes

There are plenty of potential risks with a project like this – the sheer number of letters in the BRRR acronym is a dead giveaway. Let's run through some of the main pitfalls and mistakes and how you can avoid them.

- Getting your figures wrong – Overestimating the property's market value or underestimating the cost of the building works can be fatal. Be conservative with your estimates and build in a margin for prudence.
- Buying in an area with few comparables – When it's time to remortgage, it will be harder to secure the target price you're looking for if there are few or no recent sales of comparable properties in the area. To boost your chances of success, make sure you buy in an area with enough market activity.
- Buying before a market fall – A fall in property prices in the local area will make it harder to refinance on the terms required, and your cash could be tied up for longer. Although there's no easy way to protect against this, you can avoid buying late in the property cycle and keep your projects as short

as possible. Both of these steps will reduce the chances of a general market fall affecting the outcome of your project.

- Trying to move too quickly – Although you should try to keep projects short, in most circumstances you won't be able to refinance until you've owned the property for six months or more. Make sure you build in at least six to eight months of payments on your bridging loan.

- Not having a cash buffer or contingency fund – This type of strategy tends to attract investors who are looking to stretch their investment capital further. However, things can and will go wrong on complex projects like this, and you don't want to run out of cash midway through.

Before you embark on a venture like this, make sure you think through all the things that could go wrong and have a plan in place to deal with each scenario. It will take some of the stress out of the project and help you make better decisions when problems and challenges do inevitably arise.

Keys to success

We've covered some of the keys to success as we've gone through the details of this play. However, there are some additional things you can do to maximise your chances of success with BRRR projects. Here are a few more of my top tips.

- Consider a range of scenarios – If there are a range of refurbishment options available to you, consider modelling each scenario separately and see which one gives you the best potential outcome.

- Prepare some sensitivity analysis – The final outcome of a BRRR project can be susceptible to changes in the variables, including the development costs, financing costs, and the market value at refinancing. You can use sensitivity analysis to show how both the cash left in the deal and the ROI might change as these key variables change. This can be useful for ballparking the range of potential outcomes and making sure the project is likely to be a success, even if one or more of the key variables goes against you in the execution.

- Marketing the property early – When the refurb is nearing its end, you should start marketing the property or ask your letting agent to start promoting the property to prospective tenants. The income generated will help cover the cost of the bridging loan until the refinancing is complete.

- Don't leave the refinancing to chance – Although it's not fully in your control, you can and should do everything in your power to demonstrate to the lender the value you've added. This will help you remortgage the property at the desired price. Supply the lender with before and after photos of the property, along with a full schedule of the works completed and their cost. There are no guarantees, but being proactive here will definitely help.

- Consider whether to go all cash – We've talked about using a bridging loan to finance your project, but if you do have the cash available, you could consider the cash-only alternative. Buying the property in cash can help you drive an even better price reduction at the outset. It also lowers the cost of the project, as you no longer have to cover the cost of bridging finance, and it can buy you time to ride out a dip in the local market, if prices do fall.

- Consider a specialist mortgage – On a similar vein to the previous point, there are some specialist mortgage products in the market precisely for this kind of project. These are products where the lender provides a loan based on the original purchase price, then agrees to advance you funds based on the new higher value once you've completed the works. The interest rates tend to be lower than bridging finance, and it saves you paying two sets of fees.

- Have a back-up plan – It's worth considering and fleshing out a plan B, if you can't refinance on the terms you need to make the project a success. If you're not prepared to leave your cash tied up in the investment, you could consider selling the property. If you're right about the property's market value, you should see a healthy profit on sale.

Finally, it's also worth noting that the financing products available are constantly evolving, so if you're planning on making BRRR a core part of strategy, make sure you have access to a good broker with strong ties to this market and stay on top of the latest developments. Better still, involve your broker in the planning to see if they can add some value. I promise you won't regret it.

Redux

The basic idea behind this play can be extended to other types of deal and other property rental businesses, including holiday lets, serviced accommodation and potentially even HMOs. As such, creative investors should think about how they might use it in combination with the other strategies presented in these pages. There are also other ways to add value to a property, including things like solving a structural problem, extending the lease or solving a tricky legal issue, or simply riding out a difficult and uncertain situation, e.g. think cladding issues.

Wrap up

This is a play which requires strong numbers skills, good old fashioned graft, and the mental resilience to see each step through to completion. It's not a strategy for the faint-hearted, and there are risks you'll need to manage along the way. But as long as you're prepared to put in the hard work, this is a great way to build your portfolio. At its core, this strategy is all about stretching your capital further, and you can use it to build a larger portfolio for a fraction of the money required with basic buy-to-lets. The upfront cash requirements are actually higher than for a basic buy-to-let investment, as you'll need to cover the cost of the building works and bridging finance. But you'll get this money back on refinancing. This strategy is well-suited to investors with good refurb skills, a strong network of tradespeople, and time on their hands to carefully manage each step in the process. If your aim is to build an income stream quickly using less of your own cash savings, then BRRR might be the strategy for you.

Play # 32 – Unlocking the power of capital growth

Over the past ten years, Alan had slowly and steadily built a modest property portfolio consisting of six basic buy-to-lets and one HMO. He'd built this up the hard way – saving every pound he could spare and reinvesting his profits, and it hadn't been easy. But Alan was at an inflexion point. Some of his early buy-to-let investments were now starting to show some meaningful capital growth, and this was equity he could tap into to expand his portfolio or use as working capital to fund one-off development projects.

A rising tide lifts all boats

If you've been building your property portfolio for a number of years, then you may well be sitting on some capital gains you can tap into to finance future deals and fund further expansion. This is a simple idea and it's pretty easy to execute, but it's often ignored in the plans of new investors. I think this has something to do with the fact that the timing and magnitude of any future capital growth are uncertain, and most property investors are hands-on types who like to stay in control and make things happen. Banking on capital growth then feels like you're relying on "luck" as part of your planning, and in a sense that's true, so it doesn't sit well when you're defining your strategy. Be that as it may, using this tactic to tap into the wealth created by long-term capital growth can be a game changer when it comes to growing your portfolio. Let's take a look at how.

A worked example

This play is relatively straightforward, but there are some important steps you need to take to get it right. To illustrate how it works, let's take a look at a simple example from my own portfolio that shows the core idea at work and which gives a feel for the kind of results that are possible with this strategy.

Turning back the hands of time

Back in 2014, I bought a two-bedroom, two-bathroom apartment for £180,000 in the Northern Powerhouse. I initially used this property as my own residence, but when I moved to London in 2016, I switched to an interest only mortgage and started letting the property out to tenants. Let's take a look at the figures.

Rental income	£1,000

Monthly expenditure

Mortgage interest (3% × £135,000 ÷ 12)	£338
Service charge (£1,800 ÷ 12)	£150
Ground rent (£300 ÷ 12)	£25
Management fee (12% × £1,000)	£120
Repairs and maintenance (2.5% × £1,000)	£25
Cost of voids (£1,000 × 2 / 52 weeks)	£38
Public liability insurance (£60 p.a. ÷ 12)	£5
Marketing and tenancy set-up (£240 p.a. ÷ 12)	£20
Total expenditure	£721

Cash invested

Deposit (25% × £180,000)	£45,000
Stamp duty (2014 SDLT rates)	£1,800
Furnishing costs	£2,500
Other (e.g. survey, legal expenses, broker)	£2,500
Total cash invested	£51,800

The table above shows the rental income, monthly expenditure and cash invested in the deal back when the property was first let out in 2016. It's worth noting that I financed the investment using a 75% loan-to-value interest only mortgage at a 3% p.a. interest rate. As such, the deposit was £45,000 (25% × £180,000) and the outstanding loan was £135,000 (75% × £180,000). Take a mental note, as we'll need these figures in our calculations later.

When first let, the property was generating £1,000 of rental income versus monthly expenditure of around £721. That is, I was generating £279 of cash flow each month or around £3,348 of annual profit before tax. To see what this equates to as an ROI, we simply take the annual profit of £3,348 ÷ £51,800 (i.e. the money I put into the investment) which equals 6.4% p.a. before tax. Now, let's see what the position looks like today.

Fast forward to the present day

It's been just less than seven years since I bought the apartment and less than five since I first rented it out, but things do look a little different. The market value of the property has increased from £180,000 to £220,000; this capital growth has increased the equity I own in the property to £85,000 (that is, £220,000 less the outstanding mortgage balance of £135,000). And it's this increased equity I can tap into in order to release some funds to expand my portfolio.

The monthly profit generated by the property also looks a little different. The rental income has increased from £1,000 to £1,100, but so too have my monthly expenses, which have increased from £721 to £776. What's driven this increase? Well, my mortgage interest cost of £338 per month has stayed the same, but some of my other costs, in particular the service charge and tenancy marketing costs, have increased. Other expenses like the property management fees and the cost of voids have also increased in line with the rental income. In the middle column of the table below, I have set out a summary of the monthly profit for the property as of today, before any refinancing. For simplicity, I've combined all the monthly expenditure other than the mortgage interest cost into a single line item.

	Before refinance	After refinance
Rental income	£1,100	£1,100
Monthly expenditure		
Mortgage interest (see below)	£338	£413
Other expenditure	£438	£438
Total expenditure	£776	£851
Profit / (loss) per month	£324	£249
Property price	£220,000	£220,000
Less: Loan outstanding	£135,000	£165,000
Owner's equity	£85,000	£55,000

At the present time, before any refinancing activity, the property is generating an average monthly cash flow of £324 or £3,888 of annual pre-tax profit. I still have £51,800 of my cash invested in the property, and so my return on investment has increased to 7.5% p.a. before tax (that is, £3,888 ÷ £51,800 cash invested).

The impact of refinancing

With all of the groundwork laid, it's time for the interesting bit. I haven't actually remortgaged this property yet, as I'm still a few months away from the end of the five-year fixed rate period on my current mortgage, but let's take a look at the potential impact that refinancing could have once I'm able to do this.

In the right-hand column of the table above, I've illustrated the impact. I've assumed I will remortgage the property using a 75% loan-to-value interest only mortgage at a 3% p.a. interest rate. The new loan amount will be £165,000 (75% × £220,000) and the equity I have left in the property afterwards is £55,000 (i.e. 25% × £220,000). After using the new loan of £165,000 to pay off the original loan of £135,000, the refinancing will allow me to release £30,000 in cash.

What impact will the refinancing have on my monthly profit and my return on investment? Well, my mortgage interest will increase to £413 per month (3% × £165,000 ÷ 12) and my profit will decrease to £249 per month or £2,988 per year before tax. But this is only part of the story. As we saw in the previous play, we need to look at the cash left in the deal to assess the final ROI.

Total cash invested before refinancing	£51,800
Less: Money received from new loan (75% × £220,000)	(£165,000)
Plus: Repayment of original loan (75% ×£180,000)	£135,000
Total cash invested after refinancing	£21,800

So, I originally invested £51,800 in the investment, but the refinancing will allow me to take £30,000 of cash out. That leaves me with just £21,800 of my cash tied up in the property after refinancing. The revised ROI is 13.7% p.a. before tax (that is, £2,988 profit ÷ £21,800 cash invested).

Despite the increase in my mortgage interest cost and the reduction in my monthly profit, the refinancing has allowed me to increase my ROI for the original investment (via the increased leverage), and it's allowed me to extract some cash to fund future property investments. Once the extra profit from these new investments is taken into account, I should be in a better cash flow position than before the refinancing. For the sceptics amongst you, let's take a moment to prove this. Suppose I can generate an ROI of 6% p.a. on the £30,000 extracted. If this were the case, then investing the £30,000 in a new property deal would generate an additional £150 per month (6% × £30,000 ÷ 12) to add to the £249 per month from my first investment, giving £399 per month in total from both investments. This is £75 of extra profit per month compared with the £324 per month I was making before refinancing.

Finally, it's worth noting that these figures only work if the ROI you achieve when you reinvest the cash extracted is high enough. That is, to make this play worthwhile, you need to be confident that the ROI you can achieve is significantly in excess of the mortgage interest rate on the refinanced property.

Keys to success

As with all of these strategies, there are some important things you need to do to get it right. Here are a few of the keys to success with this play:

- Timing is everything – With this strategy, you're not doing anything to force appreciation, you're simply letting time and the market do the work for you. In general, you'll want to wait until there's sufficient growth in the property's market value for the whole exercise to be worthwhile, considering the time and costs involved in the refinancing.

- The rental income needs to support the higher borrowing – Because you're increasing your borrowing, your monthly mortgage payments will increase. Lenders need to see a certain level of "rental cover" and most insist that the rental income must be at least 125% of the mortgage payment, but assessed using a higher interest rate of at least 5.5% p.a. This ratio of the rental income to monthly mortgage payments is known as the *interest coverage ratio* (or ICR). The PRA lending regulations require at least 125% cover, but some lenders use a higher ICR percentage, e.g. 135% or 145%. Your cash flow also needs to be positive and have a good margin for safety.

- Invest across a range of areas – The level of capital growth that a particular property can expect to achieve is inherently uncertain, as is the timeframe over which this will play out. Because of this, investors relying on this play to expand their portfolios should invest across a range of different locations and property types in the early stages of building their portfolio, to increase the odds that one or more of the properties will experience some level of capital growth over the short to medium term.

- Use a good mortgage broker – I've made this point before, but I would always recommend using a good mortgage broker when you're going through any kind of refinance. A good broker will help you get the best rate possible and can help you model the impact of refinancing on your monthly profits across the various loan-to-value options you might be considering.

- Watch out for early repayment charges – When you remortgage with a new provider (as opposed to a product transfer with the existing lender) you're using the new loan to pay back the previous lender. If you're still in a fixed-rate period, then any refinancing may be subject to early repayment charges. Make sure you take these charges into account in your figures or wait until after this period has expired before going through with the remortgage.
- If you can't refinance, think about selling – If you can't get the lender to agree to the valuation you want, you could think about selling up. If the property is really worth what you think it is, you should be able to sell it, cash in your equity and reinvest the proceeds. The downside of this approach is that you may be selling a perfectly good rental unit all for a modest increase in your monthly cashflow. The alternative is to wait a few years and try again.

It's worth pointing out that the rental cover test discussed in the second bullet doesn't apply to lending on more specialist property investments like commercial property, HMOs and holiday lets. This is worth bearing in mind, if you're thinking about using this play in combination with some of the other property investment types covered in these pages. In addition, the test doesn't apply to lending with a fixed term of five years or more.

Redux

Remortgaging a property to extract cash for reinvestment purposes is only one potential use of your capital gains. Let's take a look at a couple of others.

Remortgaging to increase your cash flow

Rather than refinancing at the same loan-to-value (say 75% LTV) and extracting some or all of your cash, you could consider refinancing at a lower loan-to-value (say 65% or below). The lower LTV may give you access to a lower interest rate, which could in turn allow you to improve your monthly cash flow.

For example, let's take another look at the worked example. I now own 38.6% of the equity in the property (that is, £85,000 ÷ £220,000), so I might be able to transfer onto a 65% LTV product. For illustration, if that product allows me to lower my interest rate from 3.0% p.a. to 2.7% p.a., then it could save me £34 in interest each month (0.3% p.a. × £135,000 ÷ 12, assuming I keep my borrowing at £135,000) and improve my monthly cash flow by just less than half of the £75 extra I might achieve if I reinvested the cash extracted under the first option we considered. If extra cash flow is actually what you're after, and you're not looking to grow and manage a large property portfolio, you may prefer this option.

Using your equity opportunistically

In Volume 1 of the Playbook, we discussed how to use a second mortgage charge to borrow against the equity you've accrued in a property, be that an investment property or your own home. When you take out a second mortgage charge, you receive a cash sum, the loan amount, from the lender, and you agree to repay the loan over a specified term. The loan is secured against the equity you've accrued in the property. The interest rate, though higher than you would pay on a first mortgage, is likely to be lower than for a bridging loan, so it can be a cost-effective way to fund any one-off projects you have planned.

For example, you could use the cash sum raised in this way as a pool of starter capital to finance property flips or to secure the extra funds you need to finance your next BRRR project. You might also use it (perhaps combined with any other savings you have available) to purchase a property outright in cash, rather than using a bridging loan, e.g. to fund an auction purchase. Overall, leaving a decent chunk of equity in one or more of your properties that you can access as and when you need via a second mortgage charge is a great way to build some optionality into your strategy, rather than having all your investment capital tied up 100% of the time. After all, if the deal of a lifetime crossed your path tomorrow, it's no use at all if you don't have the ability to take advantage of it.

Play # 33 – Buying property below market value (BMV)

When Peter started investing in property several years ago, it was all new to him. Being an accountant, he was great with the numbers, and his scrutiny of the likely returns from each deal had allowed him to make some sensible investments that provided good cash flow. He was pleased with his progress, but he wondered what else he could do to speed things up. At a networking event, a fellow investor challenged Peter around the quality of the deals he was making, arguing that by not pushing hard for below market value deals, he was "leaving money on the table", money that could be used to grow his portfolio quicker. Peter wondered whether this idea could be the answer.

Not another three letter acronym

There's lots of talk in property investment circles about buying below market value (or BMV). This fascination with BMV property deals appears to stem from the idea that buying below market value can help you grow your portfolio quicker by "baking in equity from day one". Personally, I blame Robert Kiyosaki of Rich Dad Poor Dad fame and some of the other property guru types out there for all their talk about no money down deals. And whilst it's certainly true that buying below market is theoretically possible and it can help you to grow your portfolio quicker, it's by no means an easy thing to do. In this play, we're going to look at what a BMV deal is, what it's not, and show how buying BMV can help you.

An introduction to BMV property

BMV deals are possible

To buy a property below market value first requires knowledge of the property's market value. This is generally defined as the estimated sale price of a property agreed between a willing buyer and a willing seller; it assumes that the property is marketed properly and that each party is fully aware of the characteristics of the property being sold. Crucially, it assumes that neither party is in an undue hurry to achieve a quick sale that could distort the final sale price.

To see why buying below market value is possible, it's useful to take a look at where the definition above might not hold in practice. Firstly, that would include any circumstances where the seller is keen to achieve a quick sale, for example a seller facing repossession or a seller undergoing a stressful event, like dealing with a bereavement and wrapping up the sale of a property as part of settling a family estate. Secondly, it would also include situations where the property has not been marketed well, which is more common than you'd think, thereby forcing the seller to reduce the price in order to achieve a sale. In these situations, buying property below market value is very much possible.

…but don't believe all the hype

At this point, it's worth acknowledging that there is a degree of subjectivity in all of this too. The market value of a property is an estimate, not an absolute fact. And all valuations are ultimately just opinions, as they're based on assumptions – even a professional valuation carried out by a qualified surveyor is only expected to be accurate to within 10 per cent of the final sale price achieved, with the acceptable bracket being larger than this in more challenging circumstances. As such, it's important to take what most investors, estate agents and marketing companies say about market value and BMV opportunities with a pinch of salt. Yes, it's all about securing a property for the cheapest possible price, but you need to ignore all the hype and make up your own mind on what's a good deal for you, given your own goals and objectives.

How buying BMV helps you

There are two ways that buying BMV can help your investment progress, one in the short term and one in the medium to long term. Let's look at these.

1. Buying BMV will improve your financials – Firstly, securing the property for lower than its market value will help improve the financials on whatever deal you're considering next. If you're looking for another buy-to-let investment or holiday rental, then buying BMV will improve your yield and your ROI. Likewise, if you're thinking about flipping properties for a profit, then buying BMV will increase the amount of profit you make from the project. This is the immediate short-term benefit of buying a property BMV, and it's available to you from day-one, without any waiting necessary.

2. It builds instant equity you can tap into later – Secondly, securing a property BMV will build immediate equity from day-one. Say for example you manage to buy a property worth £200,000 for around £180,000, at a 10% discount to its market value. Assuming you financed the deal using a 75% loan-to-value mortgage, you will have put down a deposit of £45,000 and taken out a loan for £135,000. However, because the property is really worth £200,000, you actually own £65,000 of equity on day-one (£200,000 less your outstanding loan of £135,000). This is equity you'll be able to tap into later (say when you remortgage) to expand your portfolio, as we discussed in our last play.

In practice, any equity you generate by buying BMV will likely be tied up in the property for several years. That's because it will be almost impossible to get your lender's surveyor (who's likely to err on the cautious side with their valuation) to agree that the property you just bought for £180,000 is really worth £200,000. If you're combining this play with one or more of the others, a light refurbishment say, then you may be able to justify an immediate increase in the market value. Otherwise, you'll need to wait at least a couple of years to extract this equity.

Where to find BMV deals

There are lots of ways to buy property BMV and plenty of places you can hunt for deals. Common strategies include investing in repossessions, buying property at auction, using a property sourcer and many others. With most of these, there's usually some advantage you're leveraging to secure the property BMV in the first place, be that an ability to complete a deal quickly, bulk purchasing power, or taking advantage of a network of contacts. There's lots to talk about with each of these strategies, so we're going to spend the next few chapters looking at each of these in turn and how they work. For now, we'll leave our discussion of BMV property there.

Reversal

If you can achieve it, buying property below market value is one of the best things you can do to help grow your portfolio and your wealth. However, these deals are hard to achieve (after all, why would anybody willingly sell their property for less than it's worth) and they're certainly less common than the property gurus may lead you to believe. So, to provide some counterbalance, I want to stress that you shouldn't let an obsession with buying BMV hold you back and prevent you from investing at all. In the long run, buying a good rental unit at a fair price is still likely to be a positive for your finances, and it's usually better to take some action than none at all. At a certain point, you need to stop obsessing over getting the best deal possible and simply make a move. There's a quote from Warren Buffet that's relevant here – "it's far better to buy a wonderful company at a fair price than a fair company at a wonderful price". Put slightly differently, it's important not to let an obsession with low prices and BMV deals prevent you making an otherwise great investment.

Play # 34 – Repossessed property (BMV strategy # 1)

Alfie had always been a bit of a wheeler-dealer. Early in his career, he'd run a number of stalls across popular market towns in the North; later on, he had branched out into bricks and mortar retail. He was keen to get into property as a way to diversify his income and find a safe home for his wealth. He found himself attracted to repossessions, which offered the potential for BMV deals. He'd built his retail career on the back of striking great deals, so why would his approach to property be any different?

Where angels fear to tread

Our next play, which is all about buying repossessed property, is the first of our BMV strategies. It's not unusual to see repossessed property sell between 10% and 30% below market value, so it can be a great way to grab a property bargain and accrue some instant equity from day-one. However, although there's nothing inherently risky about buying repossessed property, there are some things that you need to be aware of if you're going to get this strategy right. In this section, we're going to take a look at the property repossession process and how it works, then we're going to move on to talk about the keys to success with this approach. This is an exciting space to play in for adventurous property investors who are intent on achieving a discount to help them grow their portfolio faster, and I hope it's one you'll consider adding to your own repertoire.

How do repossessions work?

If the owner of a property, whether that be a homeowner or a buy-to-let landlord, is unable to make the repayments on a debt secured on that property, then the lender (usually a bank or building society) can repossess the property. Banks and lenders usually offer a period of grace to allow the owner to recover the situation, but sooner or later, if the debts remain outstanding, the bank or lender will make an application to the courts for a repossession order. The property will then be listed for sale on the open market.

The proceeds of the sale will go towards clearing the former owner's arrears. If the sale price achieved (less selling expenses) is greater than the outstanding mortgage debt, then the previous owner will receive the balance, subject to any other charges or interests in the property. The lender selling the repossessed property has a legal duty to achieve the best possible price. However, in practice, the lender usually wants a quick sale, and they are concerned first and foremost with recovering enough funds to repay the outstanding loan. As such, the short timeframe can mean opportunities for the astute investor.

Where to find repossession deals

In general, banks and lenders looking to sell a repossessed property tend to sell through an estate agent or at a property auction. In addition, the lender may also appoint an LPA (Law of Property Act) receiver to take control of the property and act on their behalf to recover any monies.

Although it's not always the case, it's fairly typical for individual repossessions (e.g. homeowners who fall into arrears) to be handled directly by estate agents and for investment properties (e.g. buy-to-let landlords who default on a buy-to-let mortgage) to be handled by an LPA receiver. Any properties that fall between the cracks and aren't successfully sold through an estate agent often end up being sold by an auction house or by one of the specialist vendors that have sprung up in the age of the internet to deal with repossessions. There's a growing number of companies operating in this space.

It's worth saying that when repossessed properties are being sold by an estate agent, it's not always obvious that they *are* repossessions, and that's deliberate. Most estate agents will do their best to make the property look like any other property on their books, in an attempt to secure the highest price they can get. However, there are some tell-tale signs that a property is in fact a repossession. Firstly, there's usually the strange-looking listing page, which will often include words like "we advise that an offer has been made for the above property in the sum of £158,000; any persons wishing to increase on this offer should notify the agents of their best offer prior to exchange of contracts". That's because the agent will be asked to continue to market the property right up until the sale is legally binding – that is, up until the exchange of contracts. Secondly, when you're doing viewings, a repossession will often stick out like a sore thumb. There might be metal grates or wooden boards over the windows or doors; sinks, baths and showers may have 'do not use' tape across them to make sure no-one accidently turns them on; there might also be chattels or other notices in the windows giving the former owners notice to collect any personal belongings. If you're unsure, you can simply ask the agent to confirm that it is a repossession.

It's also a requirement that repossessions are accompanied by a public notice, which is usually done by way of a listing in a local newspaper. Once you know which local papers the agents use to list public notices, this can be a great way to spot new deals coming on to the market. Again, if you don't know which papers they use, call the agents up and ask them.

Spotting repossessed properties at auction is usually a little easier, but it's still not always straightforward. When you're looking through an auction catalogue, you should look for phrases like "by order of the mortgagee" or "by order of the receiver". These are clear signals the property is a repossession. If you suspect a property is a repossession, but it's not clear in the catalogue, you can contact the seller's solicitor and ask them for the background to the sale. This should give you an answer, but it is a time-consuming process that's not easy to automate. That's why many investors adopting this strategy prefer to work with auction houses specialising in repossessed properties.

Keys to success

Buying a repossessed property is a slightly different investment proposition. The property you're buying has a different kind of backstory, and that brings some nuances you'll need to manage. Here are some of my top tips.

- Expect the property to be in poor condition – Not all repossessed properties are in poor condition, but many are. The property is unlikely to have received the right level of care before it was repossessed, and the lender or receiver will have done the minimal level of work required prior to sale. You need to carefully assess the cost of any repairs and refurbishment works needed and factor these into your offer. If you can, take your builder out to view the property with you to help you assess the likely cost, and insist on a second viewing – you may not spot everything the first time around.

- Coping with a lack of information – When buying a repossession, there may be less information available to you than with a typical sale process. This is especially likely to be the case when a receiver has been brought in to handle the sale – it wouldn't be uncommon for a receiver to provide no replies at all to buyer inquiries, so this will restrict the amount of due diligence you can perform. In light of this, you'll want to get a more comprehensive survey done than you normally would, to ensure there are no defects, and you'll want your solicitor to look over the legal pack to make sure there's no weakness in the title and to spot any other potential legal problems.

- Watch out for hidden costs – There are a variety of hidden costs to watch out for when buying repossessed property. It's likely that some (if not all) of the utility services have been cut-off and these will require reinstating. There's a cost involved in doing this. You should also check the legal pack or ask your solicitor to confirm there are no unpaid charges, e.g. unpaid service charges or ground rents. These should have been dealt with by the lender prior to the sale, but it's important to check this is in fact the case. You're not responsible for the previous owner's debts.

- Dealing with a sitting tenant – If the repossessed property was a buy-to-let, then you should check whether the sitting tenants have handed over the keys and vacated the property. This situation should have been resolved by the mortgagee and owner, before the property was made available for sale, but it's important to clarify the position. Ideally, you would want to buy the property vacant, as this will give you the time and space to carry out any refurbishment works needed. However, properties are sometimes sold with a tenant in place or in situ, in which case you may need to wait until the end of the current tenancy to get in and do the works.

- Factor in the potential for gazumping – Usually when you buy a property, it's taken off the market when your offer is accepted, giving you time and space to complete your due diligence and for your solicitor to take care of the legal aspects of the purchase. When you buy a repossessed property, the seller is under a legal duty to the previous owner to get the maximum price they can, meaning that even after your offer is accepted, the property will continue to be marketed until exchange of contracts. That means it's possible for another buyer to come along midway through the process and offer more, at which point their offer will be accepted and yours rejected, and any fees you've incurred to this point, e.g. broker fees, legal expenses, or survey costs, will be lost. If buying repossessed property is a core part of your property strategy, you should expect to write off costs like this from time to time. Alternatively, you could stick to auction purchases where the likelihood of irrecoverable costs is somewhat reduced (more on that in our next play).

- Have your financing lined up in advance – If you're buying through an agent, you'll want to get the deal finalised as quickly as you can in order to reduce the potential for gazumping. Likewise, if you're buying at auction, you'll need to complete the sale within 28 days (or less) of your offer being accepted. Because of this, you'll want to have your financing lined up in advance before striking any deals. In general, this means you'll want to buy in cash or using bridging finance, as a mortgage will be too slow here.

- Check the deal is BMV – Just because the property is a repossession doesn't mean it's a great deal. You'll want to verify early on that the deal has legs and construct your offer accordingly. You should use the *comparison method of valuation* (which we discussed in detail in play # 25 of Volume 1) and check the sold prices from HM Land Registry for comparable properties in the area to confirm that you are in fact getting a BMV deal. When you're doing this, you should carefully factor in all the costs you're likely to incur in bringing the property back up-to-scratch.

- Manage the impact on your credit score – After you purchase the property, you should carefully monitor your credit score (using one of the free online credit services) and watch out for payment demands from debt collection agencies. You want to make sure that the previous owner's debts don't affect your credit rating. If you do receive any payment demands, call the sender to explain that this individual no longer lives at the address, and return any letters to the senders. It's important to know that you're not responsible for the former owner's debts, regardless of who's trying to collect. If bailiffs try to enter the property, then you'll need to explain the situation, and you'll likely need to confirm your identity and prove that you're the new owner of the property, so keep this paperwork handy.

Redux

If this all sounds a bit too scary, there are ways to get some of the advantages of buying a repossession, without the downsides. One of these is to consider buying *pre-repossession property* as an alternative. A pre-repossession property is one where the owner has fallen into arrears, perhaps by one or two months, but where the lender has not yet sought a repossession order. In these circumstances, you might be able to strike a deal to buy the property, allowing the existing owner to clear their debts and stop the lender repossessing. To find these opportunities, speak to local agents directly or work with a specialist company that markets these kinds of deals.

Play # 35 – Buying property at auction (BMV strategy # 2)

William, known as Billy to his friends and business associates, was a regular in the auction rooms. Billy ran a family building company and was always on the lookout for new opportunities. When work dried up and his firm had excess capacity, Billy would create his own work by scouting auction houses for properties to flip and refurbishment projects he could pitch to investors. Every once in a while, he would keep a property or two for his own portfolio. For Billy, none of this would have been possible without buying at auction.

Why buy property at auction

This next play, which is all about buying property at auction, is the second of our BMV strategies. It's not unusual to see auction properties sell between 15% and 35% below the prices they may have achieved with an estate agent, so it can be a great way to grab a property bargain. It's also an exciting and efficient way to buy property, as once the hammer falls on a winning bid, that bidder is contractually bound to buy the property. In practice, that means all the work involved in buying at auction is front-end loaded, and your research and due diligence needs to be completed before you enter the auction room. But it's not all glitz and glamour and Homes Under the Hammer, buying at auction also comes with some real risks that you'll need to manage along the way. In this play, we're going to look at how buying property at auction works and at some of the keys to success.

A crash course in property auctions

Before we get into the detail of how to buy property at auction, how to increase your chances of success, and how to manage the key risks, it's useful to step back and get an overview of what property auctions are all about. So, we're first going to take a look at why people choose to sell at auction, at some auction terminology you need to know, and at the costs involved in buying at auction.

Why people sell at auction

There's always a reason a property is being sold at auction, and it's important you find this out to see if it's a dealbreaker. Common reasons are as follows.

- The owner needs a quick sale – Sometimes the vendor will be looking for a quick sale, e.g. for personal or financial reasons. Selling at auction offers these vendors a guaranteed way to sell within a specified timeframe.
- The property needs work doing – The properties you'll see at auction range from wrecks to light refurbishment projects. Damage to the property can be superficial or serious structural damage. Sometimes it can be difficult to tell.
- It's a repossession – It's often the case that repossessions that fail to sell via an agent will end up in an auction. This allows mortgagees to demonstrate they've sold the property at the highest price and to prove accountability.
- The vendor is a public body – Public bodies like Local Authorities also need to demonstrate that they've achieve the highest possible sale price for any properties they sell. Auctions are a simple and transparent way to do this.
- The property has a legal issue – If a property has a legal issue, such as a short lease, a title problem, or an absentee freeholder, then it may be more difficult to sell through an estate agent, and it may end up in an auction as a result.
- The property is unique or in a remote location – Auctions can be a great way to sell properties that are unique, difficult to value, or in remote locations. Think development sites, lighthouses, or run-down castles in Scotland.

Remember, there's always a reason a property is being sold at auction – if you can't spot it, that makes the purchase riskier. The problem may be something that affects your ability to raise finance and could prevent you reselling the property. Your job is to play detective, work out what the problem is, and factor the costs of putting it right into your bid.

Need-to-know auction parlance

Like any specialist activity, auctions have their own terminology and phrases that you need to understand. Here are a few of the basics.

o   Lot – This means the property or the land being sold. Each item in the auction catalogue will have its own lot number.
o   Guide price – The guide price is set by the auction house and it gives potential buyers an idea of what they might expect to pay for a property.
o   Reserve price – This is the lowest price that the seller is willing to accept for the property. Sometimes it's disclosed by the seller, but usually it's not.
o   Bid – A bid is an official offer, a proposal to purchase the property at the price that's put forward. Once a bid is made and accepted, it's legally binding.
o   Legal pack – This pack will contain documents like the 'conditions of sale', 'special conditions', title deed and plan, lease agreement and any 'searches'.

It's also worth knowing that even if the reserve price is not disclosed, the guide price can give you some indication. This is because guide prices are usually set within 5% to 10% of the reserve price. Just knowing this can give you some idea of the minimum price that the vendor will accept. If a property does not reach the reserve price, the property will not be sold.

Costs involved in the buying process

The costs involved in buying a property at auction are similar to buying via an estate agent, but there are some auction-specific costs you should know about. In addition to the purchase price, stamp duty, legal expenses, survey and valuation fees, and other finance-related costs, you'll also incur the following costs:

- Buyer's premium – This fee is payable by the buyer to the auction house. It's often called an 'administration fee' or 'auction house fee'. It can be a fixed fee, say £250 to £750, or a percentage of the final sale price, e.g. 1% or 2%.
- Seller's legal expenses – It's becoming increasingly common for sellers to ask buyers to cover a portion of their legal costs, e.g. up to a certain percentage of the sale price. You should watch out for additional costs like this.

We've covered the analysis needed and how to approach the calculations for buy-to-let investments, light refurbishments and BRRR deals in previous plays. We've also covered the calculations and sensitivity analysis you'll need when flipping properties for a profit. When buying at auction, you simply need to factor in the additional costs above into your analysis, when running your numbers.

Keys to success

Before TV shows like Homes Under the Hammer came along, auction houses were the domain of specialist investors. And although these TV programmes have done wonders to raise the profile of property auctions and make them accessible, they haven't educated would-be buyers about the risks of buying at auction or how to manage these. In this section, we'll look at some of the keys to success and best practices when buying at auction.

How to find auction properties

There are three main ways to find auction property. The first is via the websites of the auction houses themselves. If you get in touch with me, I can send you my list of all the auction houses in the UK, along with details of the auction area they serve and a link to their website. Some of the websites provide free email updates on new property listings when they hit the market, and this can be a cheap source of information for property investors that are new to buying at auction and who don't yet want to shell out for the cost of a subscription service. If you want to receive a copy of my list, then make sure you check out the free resources section at the end of the book.

The second way to find auction property for sale is to sign up to a professional subscription service like that offered by Essential Information Group. EIG offers a full listing of all auction houses and properties sold in the UK, as well as some useful information on recently sold lots. It's an online resource that charges an annual membership fee (of around £300 to £400 per year) and it can be a great resource for property investors that are serious about buying at auction. Further details can be found at www.eigpropertyauctions.co.uk – you'll need to contact their sales team for the current price of their annual subscription.

The third and final way to find auction properties is to sign up to the mailing lists of any auction houses you intend to frequent. These mailing lists will update you on upcoming auction dates and send through auction catalogues, once these are available. Many of the large auction houses are based in London, but they will often sell properties from across the UK, so you should make sure you check these out too, even if you are restricting your purchases to a particular area.

Work the auction catalogue

Once you have a copy of the auction catalogue, you can work your way through to see if there are any properties of interest. The catalogue entry itself will contain basic information like the address, one or two photographs, and a usually a brief description of the property being sold, including details of the number of rooms, the size of the property, whether it's leasehold or freehold, whether it's vacant or tenanted, and who's selling the property. The catalogue will also provide details of the guide price and the viewing arrangements.

With this basic information on the property in hand, you should move on to some desktop research. You can check out the location of the property on Google Maps, including using the aerial view to confirm its boundaries and its proximity to transport links, employment centres, schools and shops, and you can even take a virtual walk down the street to get a feel for the area using Google Map's Street View function. You can also check out recent sold prices for similar properties (or sometimes the actual property) on the Land Registry and check out the portals, like Rightmove and Zoopla, to see if there are additional photos of the property held on there from past listings. If you're still interested after this, you should take a look at the legal pack put together by the auction house.

Check the legal pack

Most auction houses allow potential buyers to download the legal pack from their website or will send this across by email or post on request. Even though you're not a lawyer, it's vital you read the legal pack first before taking any further action to understand what it is you're buying and the terms of the sale. The legal pack should contain copies of the title deed and title plan, a copy of the lease where you can check the lease length and ground rent provisions, searches (like local authority, environmental, drainage and water, coal mining and other searches) and the Energy Performance Certificate. There will also be 'conditions of sale' and 'special conditions' documents you should read. These documents, particular the latter, will set out the key terms of the sale, and it's where you will find any special terms, e.g. completion within 14 days, buyers needing to cover the seller's legal expenses, and other onerous terms you need to know about. The legal pack also contains useful information on historical service charges and, if the property is tenanted, a copy of the tenancy agreement. If not provided, you should ask the auction house for an up-to-date rental statement, to see if the tenant is in arrears and has missed any payments.

Make the most of viewings

Viewings for auction properties are a little bit different than when buying with an estate agent. There is usually only a limited number of viewings before the auction, and viewings will usually be arranged as block viewings for all interested buyers to attend. The person conducting the viewing won't necessarily have any details about the property, so it's up to you to make the most of the time available and to gather all the information you need on your own. You won't have long, and there will be other interested parties milling around the property too.

There can be a lot to evaluate in a short space of time, so you need to write down all the information you need to assess any works needed and put together your bid. You should also take good photographs that you can refer back to later. You'll need to understand the condition of the roof, inspect the ceilings for any evidence of leaks, check out the plumbing and state of the boiler, figure out the likely age and state of the electrics and the main fuse board, check the structure of the building and straightness of the walls, watch out for any signs of movement like cracks in the walls, and confirm there are no signs of damp under the flooring or behind walls. When you're doing this, watch out for recent redecoration which might have been done to hide structural problems, damp issues and leaks. If the doors and windows don't close properly, this might indicate structural problems. You also need to assess the size of rooms (including bedrooms, bathrooms and kitchens) to see if standard-sized items will fit and check that any changes to the property have planning permission. Outside the property, check that the space and boundary lines are as per the title plan, document any maintenance required, and confirm the parking arrangements are as you expect.

If you're new to all this, you might want to take a trusted builder around the property with you when you view it, so they can help you assess the likely cost of works and to spot potential opportunities to add value, e.g. through changes to the layout or by adding extra space. A good builder will be able to help you assess the general condition of the property, cost repairs, and offer practical advice and guidance on any problems you encounter, when viewing the property.

Build the investment case

After you've viewed the property, you'll likely have just a couple of weeks to build the investment case and get things in place for the big day. This is a crucial period of time where you need to press forward with your due diligence, decide whether or not to bid on the property and at what price, and tidy up any loose ends. There are a number of key things you'll need to do over this period to be in a position to bid for the property on auction day. Let's take a closer look at these now.

- Prepare your modelling and bid limits – You need to use all the information you've gathered via your research and at the viewing to cost out any works needed and prepare your valuation model. Use the model to decide whether the purchase has a chance of meeting your criteria (for rental properties) or your target profit (for flipping projects). If there's little chance of the deal working out, don't take it any further – just move on. If there's a chance the deal might work, set your ideal bid price and your maximum bid limit.

- Consider getting a survey – Surveys carried out by a RICS qualified surveyor can provide you with a wealth of information. If the property is a new build apartment, you might see no need for a survey. Otherwise, for any properties in reasonable condition built in the last 150 years, a homebuyer's report will likely suffice and will highlight any defects that may affect the value of the property. For properties in poor condition, which are old, unusual or of non-standard construction, or which have undergone substantial alteration, you should consider a full structural survey, which will flag any defects and issues and provide advice on how to remedy these.

- Have a solicitor review the legal pack – At this stage, it makes sense to have a solicitor review the legal pack. There are all kinds of issues that can crop up, everything from defective lease clauses and absentee freeholders to right of way or access issues and lack of planning permission for past alterations. There can be issues with incorrect, unregistered, or complicated title deeds. Some legal issues are more serious than others, but unless you're a solicitor you won't be able to tell how serious. Some can make the property unsuitable as security for a loan, effectively making the property unmortgageable.

How much input you feel you need from surveyors, builders and solicitors to get to a place where you're comfortable to bid will depend on the property you're looking at and your own level of experience and expertise. It may be possible to save on some costs, e.g. if you ask your surveyor or solicitor to provide you with a verbal rather than a written report, but if you decide to proceed to the bid stage, you shouldn't skip these steps. Yes, it might cost you a few hundred pounds in adviser fees, but that is money well spend if it saves you from making a big, costly mistake in the first place. As a ballpark on costs, you can expect to pay £300 to £400 for a homebuyer's survey, £500 to £600 for a full structural survey, and £200 to £400 for a review of the legal pack. You should also ask your solicitor if they would be willing to deduct this cost or provide a discount on their full legal costs, if your bid is successful and you use them to complete on the transaction.

Arrange your financing

When buying at auction, it's paramount that you have the funds available or that you have access to the funds to complete the transaction in a short timeframe. If your bid is successful on auction day, you'll exchange contracts immediately and you will be required to pay the deposit (usually 10% of the purchase price) there and then, as well as settle any fees due to the auctioneer. Payments are usually accepted by cheque, debit card or banker's draft, and the funds must be cleared funds. The balance is then usually due 28 days later at completion, but it's not uncommon for completion to take place after just 14 days for repossessions.

The agreement made when your bid is accepted is a legally binding contract. As a result, if you're not able to raise finance and complete within the required timescales, you'll forfeit your deposit and potentially be open to legal action from the seller, as well as other financial penalties. So, it's important you start to line up your financing before auction day. In practice, most parties buying at auction are either buying in cash or using bridging finance, as relying on a mortgage is too risky. You should work with a good broker to line up your financing before auction day so that it's prepped and ready to go. Make sure the lender is aware this is an auction purchase and get them to confirm they can meet the timeline. Also, make sure you have a back-up option in case your financing falls through.

On auction day

The big day has finally arrived, and this is no time to lose focus. Before you set off, call the auction house and make sure the lot you want to bid on is still available and hasn't been withdrawn. You should aim to arrive at the auction house two hours ahead of your lot – this will give you time to check any amendments or announcements related to the lot, all of which will form part of the final contract. You should take with you any documentation required, including photographic ID and proof of your residential address. You should check in advance what forms of payment are accepted and take these along too. If you're purchasing through a limited company, you may also need a signed letter from the Board of Directors, authorising you to bid on behalf of the company. You should keep the property details, including all paperwork, research notes, your modelling, the lot number, and your bid limits to hand, as you may want to refer back to these.

Bidding for the property

If you're still in any doubt about the property, then you should decide to drop out before you enter the auction room. It can be difficult to do this, as you will have invested time and energy and incurred some costs getting to this point, but if you have any doubts, it's best not to proceed.

In the auction room, you need to find a spot where you can see what's going on and be seen by the auctioneer. Standing at the back offers the advantage of being able to see the whole room and competing bidders, but you need to make sure you can make eye contact with the auctioneer – if he or she doesn't see your bid, you might lose out on the property. When it comes to bidding strategy, it's often best to bid late and come in right at the end. You should aim to let any early bidding wars burn themselves out and try to wait until the bidding is almost done before you come in. You're hoping for a last-minute surprise that will catch other bidders off guard. It's also worth knowing that you are free to propose smaller or larger bid increments, if you think this will help, though it's up to the auctioneer whether to accept these or not. Both can help you get to a winning bid, as larger bid increments can help disrupt the flow, and smaller bid increments can help to slow things down and push your nose ahead in the race. It can also help if the bid limits you set yourself are not round numbers. Think £66,500 and £83,250 as good examples of bid limits that might help you secure the winning bid.

Finally, the most important thing to remember is not to get carried away by the excitement of the day and the buzz of the auction room. Make sure you stick to the bidding limits that you set yourself and never overbid for a property.

What to do if you win

If you're lucky enough to put forward the winning bid (and within your bidding limits) then your work is not done yet. You'll now get to take part in the race to complete, so you're in for another hectic few weeks. On auction day itself, you'll exchange contracts and pay the deposit, but there are a few other things to take care of too. You'll need to instruct a solicitor to take over the buying process, contact your finance provider to discuss next steps, and arrange any insurances needed on the property. Technically, the property may still be covered under the seller's insurances, e.g. their buildings insurance cover. However, if the property is damaged during the period between exchange and completion, it will be easier to rectify under your own insurance policy than by making a claim to the seller's insurance company. The coming weeks will likely be just as hectic as the weeks preceding auction day, and you'll need to make calls at least every other day to your finance provider, your solicitor, and the auction house to make sure things stay on track and to remove any blockers holding up the process.

Redux

It's also possible to buy an auction property before or after auction day itself. The main reason you might want to make an offer before the auction is to secure the deal and prevent the property going to auction at all. If you do this, your offer will likely need to be in excess of the guide price, so you're taking a gamble in that you might end up paying more or less than you would have done in the room, and you might also prompt an increase in the reserve or the guide price, which can work against you, if the property does proceed to auction. You'll also need to complete the sale before the auction date, and so the pressure is still on to get the deal done quickly, and you'll need to pay the 10% deposit and the auctioneer's fees upfront, just like you would at auction. Note that this route isn't going to be possible if the vendor is a public body or a mortgagee selling a repossession, as these sellers are under an obligation to get the best possible price and need to be transparent in their dealings. This is the main reason that more properties are not sold before auction day, but it can sometimes be a good tactic.

Lastly, it's also possible to buy properties after auction day. If a property does not sell on the day, for example, if there are no bids that meet the reserve price, then it will still be available for sale afterwards as an unsold lot. In the trade, the practice of scouting auction catalogues for unsold lots is known as 'hawking'. The unsold property will usually be for sale at the reserve price that was set on the day, and it's a first-to-exchange-wins type of competition. If you miss out on your preferred lot on the day and you're looking for a consolation prize, then grabbing one of the unsold lots might be your silver lining. In all seriousness, scouting the unsold lots can be a great way to grab a property bargain, and it's another tactic you might want to add to your own playbook.

Play # 36 – Using a property sourcer (BMV strategy # 3)

Jason and his wife Lisa were both finance professionals and both travelled extensively for work. They were keen on property as an asset class, but they had little time to dedicate to sourcing property deals and managing their property portfolio. Despite what their lives looked like from the outside, it wasn't all roses, and they certainly weren't swimming in cash. They needed to source strong, preferably BMV, deals to help enhance their ROI and speed up their progress. For Jason and Lisa, it was all about finding a good property sourcer or property investment company to help them with this. They needed someone they could trust and someone who understood their strategy. They needed a partner that would save them time, not add to their workload.

Increasing your deal flow

Our next play, which is all about using a property sourcer, is the third of our BMV strategies. We briefly touched on property sourcing in play # 7 of Volume 1, but to recap, a property sourcer is anyone who goes out and finds property deals on other people's behalf and who charges a fee for their services. This could be an individual or a property investment company that sources deals for their clients. Ideally, they should have access to networks and other potential deal sources that you don't, and the deals they present should be better than you could negotiate for yourself. A strong sourcer might be able to negotiate a deal that's between 5%

and 25% below market value, so it can be a great way to build equity and wealth over the course of your property journey. What's more, for the time poor amongst you, a property sourcer can save you time and increase the volume of deals (deal flow) crossing your desk, making it easier to hit your objectives. In this play, we're going to look at how to find a property sourcer, how to vet them and choose which ones to work with, and at some of the keys to success when assessing property deals they present to you. If you can find the right fit, working with a good sourcer has the potential to supercharge your progress, and it's an approach to sourcing property deals that you might want to add into the mix.

Working with a property sourcer

How to find a property sourcer

Property sourcers come in all shapes and sizes, from well-established property investment companies who source deals for their clients to individuals working alone. But how do you go about finding one you want to work with? Well, let's take a look at five of the most common ways to find a property sourcer.

1. Work with a property investment company – There are plenty of companies out there that aim to help you invest in property. The scope of their services will differ, but typically they help you source suitable investment properties via their network of contacts and help you through the purchase process, e.g. liaising with solicitors and mortgage brokers on your behalf. Above all, you need to choose the right company to work with, and we'll come back to the vetting and selection process shortly.

2. Ask for a referral or recommendation – One of the best ways to find a sourcer is to ask for a referral or a recommendation. Ideally, this would come from someone you already trust and have an existing relationship with, someone who invests in property themselves, and someone who understands a little bit about your goals and what you're trying to achieve. Failing that, you could reach out to contacts in your network that are acquiring lots of properties

and ask how they are sourcing their deals. This might open up some extra leads and generate some additional avenues of inquiry.

3. Go to networking events – Attending networking events can be a great way to meet fellow investors and strike up a relationship with a property sourcer. This strategy is particularly good if you're looking to contact sourcers that specialise in a local area or that specialise in a particular type of investment, e.g. HMOs, holiday lets, or refurb opportunities. Trying to find a non-sleazy networking event can be hard, but you should try to attend one with a ban on any selling activity.

4. Join a social media group – Although I'm not a big fan of social media myself (I came off all social media, including LinkedIn, a couple of years back) there are property groups out there on most of the social media platforms. I would avoid any groups that publicly push specific deals, as they're usually full of sharks that would sell their own grandma for a nickel, and I'd stick to local property networking groups and groups that are dedicated to niche property strategies. These groups can be a good way to expand your network and find a sourcer, but please do be careful.

5. Build your profile at one of the property forums – Networking online at one of the property forums is a great way to meet people. Forums like Property Hub and Property Tribes are much less salesy than the social media groups, owing to bans on self-promotion. Your approach should be to share your property story and your aims and objectives via posts in the relevant topic chats and to ask for help expanding your network. Once you're a little more established, you'll also be able to Private Message (PM) people who you think might be able to help you out.

Those are just some of the ways you might go about finding a property sourcer, but there are others. Ultimately, it boils down to finding an approach that you're comfortable with and that fits with your wider approach to property.

Vetting a sourcing partner

So, with a bucket load of new contacts and some new relationships in the offing, your next step is to choose partners you want to work with in the future. For me, there are two parts to this: firstly, it's important to carry out basic background checks on anyone that you intend to work with, to establish their credibility and track record; secondly, you need to work out whether this person will be a good fit for you, given your wider goals and your strategy. Let's take a closer look at some of the things you can do to vet your new partner.

- Check if they're registered – The Property Ombudsman is a government approved scheme that provides independent redress in relation to disputes between consumers and property agents. It's fairly inexpensive to register, and so it's a low, entry-level requirement that any property sourcer should have place. If they're not registered, ask them why.

- Carry out background checks – Carrying out a Google search (search the first ten pages, not just page one) will help you unearth anything unsavoury on the web. This can be helpful when vetting property investment companies and getting a general feel for what they're all about. For individual sourcers, try to find someone who's worked with them before and ask that person about their experiences, both good and bad.

- Make sure they're an investor – It's a simple test, but you should make sure any property sourcer you're intending to work with is also an investor. If they're not, you should think twice about working with them. After all, would you trust a cook that didn't love eating their own food? Being a bit of a foodie myself, I certainly wouldn't.

- Ask to see examples of past deals they've sourced – Any sourcer worth their salt will be able to provide you with examples of past deals they've sourced. This is their portfolio, their résumé if you will, that showcases what they can do. Ideally, they would also put you in contact with the people that bought those deals, so you can see how they worked out. Failing that, you should look to verify the figures and examples they present to you, using sold prices at the Land Registry, for example. If they're making excuses, it's usually a bad sign. Ultimately, this check is all about establishing their credibility and making sure they have a track record.

- Make sure they understand your goals – If you're going to build a strong working relationship, you need to make sure they understand your strategy. If this person has no interest in your goals and your plans, then you can rest assured they're more concerned with making a buck or two and that they're simply trying to flog you something. Try to work with a sourcer that takes the time to listen and to find out what type of properties you're looking for, be that new build apartments or houses looking for a refurb.

Finally, you could always try "shopping" them, as a test of their trustworthiness. For example, you could call them up and tell them you have £200,000 to invest and see how they react. If they immediately start sending you deals, rather than getting to know you and what you're trying to achieve, then you're likely dealing with someone who's a bit of a shark.

How to assess the deals they bring to you

Assessing a deal brought to you by a property sourcer is just like assessing any other deal. However, when you're running the numbers, you need to include any fees charged by the sourcer in your deal calculations. Let's illustrate this concept with a simple example.

I'm going to build off the buy-to-let example we considered in play # 20 of Volume 1. To recap briefly, the property we considered was a two-bedroom, two-bathroom apartment close to Leeds City Centre. We estimated that if we managed to secure the flat for around £160,000, we might achieve an ROI close to 5.0% p.a. and a positive cash flow of around £208 per month, based on a rental income of £825 per month and average monthly expenditure of £617. But what if instead of sourcing the deal ourselves, we worked with a property sourcer who managed to source an equivalent apartment at a 12.5% discount to its market value. Let's take a look at how this impacts the figures.

The table below illustrates the two deals. The middle column shows the deal we sourced ourselves. We paid £160,000 for the property and financed the deal using a 75% loan-to-value interest only mortgage at a 3% p.a. interest rate. So, within the monthly expenditure of £617 is a mortgage interest cost of £300 (3% × 75% × £160,000 ÷ 12). In the deal from the sourcer, shown in the right-hand column, we pay £140,000 for the property (£160,000 less a 12.5% discount). Our mortgage interest cost falls to £263 per month (3% × 75% × £140,000 ÷ 12) assuming we use a 75% loan-to-value mortgage based off the lower price. If all the other running costs are the same, that means our monthly expenditure falls to £580 (the original monthly expenditure of £617 less our £37 saving on the mortgage interest cost). The rest of the figures then work out as follows.

	Without sourcer	With sourcer
Property price	£160,000	£160,000
Discount	0%	12.5%
Final price	£160,000	£140,000
Expected income		
Rental income	£825	£825
Monthly expenditure	£617	£580
Profit / (loss)	£208	£245
Cash invested		
– Deposit (25% × £160,000)	£40,000	£35,000
– Stamp duty	£5,500	£4,500
– Furnishing costs	£2,000	£2,000
– Valuation and survey	£500	£500
– Legal expenses	£1,500	£1,500
– Mortgage broker	£500	£500
– Sourcing fee	-	£3,600
Total cash invested	£50,000	£47,600

In the right-hand column, I've shown how the figures could look with the deal that's been sourced by our property investment company. That is, we expect to achieve £825 of rental income versus our monthly expenses of £580. We could expect to generate £245 of cash flow each month or around £2,940 of annual pre-tax profit. To see what this gives us as an ROI, we take the annual profit of £2,940 ÷ £47,600 (i.e. the money we put into the deal, including the £3,600 sourcing fee) which is an annual ROI of 6.2% before tax.

In this example, the ROI of 6.2% p.a. in the deal from our sourcer is higher than the ROI of 5.0% p.a. in the deal we sourced, so we're better off with the deal from our sourcer, even after taking into account their sourcing fee. In practice, in choosing to accept the deal or not, you should apply the same criteria, i.e. around cap rate, ROI and capital growth potential, that you would on any other deal. The fact that the deal has been sourced for you by a third party makes no difference whatsoever.

Common pitfalls and mistakes

Although working with a property sourcer has many advantages, like increasing your deal flow and getting access to better deals you couldn't negotiate yourself, there are some common pitfalls and mistakes.

- Not doing thorough due diligence yourself – One of the biggest mistakes you can make when working with a property sourcer is to trust the figures you're presented with a little too much. It's up to you to do thorough due diligence and form your own view on the numbers, including the likely rental income and running costs of the property. If you're unfamiliar with the area, you'll need to work doubly hard to make up for your lack of knowledge.

- Assuming you'll be able to secure financing – Sometimes, property sourcers will secure access to several units at the same development, say a new build development being marketed by a developer. If too many units are likely to be sold to investors, banks and lenders can sometimes refuse to lend on the property, and this can lead to problems raising finance. You should speak to a broker in advance and make sure you'll have financing options available.

- Not understanding the deal – Is the property on offer a new build that will require flooring and white goods that aren't included in the price? Will the property be acquired with a tenant in situ or with vacant possession? You need to fully understand the facts and circumstances around the deal, so that you can model the returns properly and understand what you're buying. If your sourcer doesn't have answers, make sure they get them for you.

- Feeling obliged to say yes – Just because your sourcing partner has worked hard to put a deal together doesn't mean you should feel obliged to say yes. If this deal isn't right for you or doesn't meet your criteria, you should politely decline. Remember the Warren Buffett quote that "the difference between successful people and really successful people is that really successful people say 'no' to almost everything". Property investment is no different.

- Not having a contract – Not putting a contract in place with your sourcing partner and relying on trust alone can be a costly mistake. Most property investment companies will have a standard contract they want you to sign, which you should review thoroughly. With an individual sourcer, you should look to get some kind of agreement in place which sets out the obligations of each party. Ideally, the sourcing fee would be paid across to the sourcer only when the deal is legally secured, on exchange of contracts, but there are times when this can be relaxed, such as when you're working with a trusted partner or when exchange is expected in a matter of days.

As a final word of caution, there are plenty of sharks out there in the property industry, and some of them work as sourcers. You need to be able to spot them for what they are and avoid them. It's up to you to know exactly who you're doing business with and take the necessary steps and precautions to safeguard your money, your reputation and your time. So, tread cautiously, and make sure you follow the guidance and advice in this play.

Reversal

There are investors out there who are excellent at deal sourcing and who come across more opportunities than they have capacity for themselves. If you fall into this category, and, if you have sufficient time on your hands to make the most of this opportunity, then you could consider starting a property sourcing business of your own. Any sourcing fees you generate can be used to supplement your property income and speed up your investment progress. You'll need to set this up properly, including getting registered with The Property Ombudsman, putting the right business and legal processes in place and learning how to source and structure deals on behalf of your clients. Even more crucially, you'll need to build up a network of investors who are keen to do the kinds of deals that you're able to source. Property sourcing is a business in its own right, but for those with a natural talent for deal making and who love the hunt, this can be a great way to earn some extra income.

Play # 37 – Buying property off plan (BMV strategy # 4)

Alberto worked for one of the big UK property developers as a regional sales manager. From time to time, usually at the start of the development cycle, the company would offer discounts to buyers that were willing to take units early or in bulk; likewise, in the latter stages of a development, the company was often willing to let the last few units go for a great price, in order to meet their year-end sales targets. Over the years, Alberto regularly put his money where his mouth was, snapping up properties opportunistically when great deals were on offer. He knew good value when he saw it.

Getting in early doors

This next play, which is about buying off plan property, is the fourth of our BMV strategies. But what is 'off plan' property? Simply put, an off plan property is a property that hasn't been built yet, so you're buying the property 'off the plan'. The developer is still building the property (or perhaps they haven't started yet), and they're selling it to you early doors before it's completed and ready-to-buy, which can bring the potential for discounts and good deals. However, the off plan period itself can span a long time, with off plan deals ranging from properties where construction is largely complete and completion is just a couple of weeks away, to deals where completion might be two years away and where the spade hasn't hit the ground. Because of this, there are unique risks and opportunities you need to be aware of, if you're going to buy off plan, and it's an area where even experienced investors can lose money, if they're not careful. In this play, we're going to look at the process for buying off plan, at some of the upsides and downsides, and at how you can manage the key risks involved.

How to buy property off plan

Before we get into the upsides and the downsides, it's worth taking a step back to look at why these deals exist and at the buying process itself. There are three main reasons why developers choose to sell property off plan:

1. It helps their cash flow – Early in the build, developers will be keen to create positive cash flow by selling some units. Yes, that means they're potentially using your deposit to fund the development, which brings its own risks.
2. It de-risks the build – No developer wants to get to the end of a build and be stuck with lots of units they can't sell. As such, selling some of the units early can de-risk the build and leave less money at risk in the latter stages.
3. To stoke demand – Developers are keen to demonstrate to buyers that the development is in demand. With a certain percentage of units 'sold out', this can help them drive up demand and secure higher prices on later sales.

So, that's a little bit about the developer's perspective. But how does the buying process work? Let's run through the key steps you'll need to go through when you're buying a property off plan:

- Pay the reservation fee – The first step in buying property off plan is to pay a reservation fee to the developer to secure the deal. This fee is typically in the range £1,000 to £5,000 and can usually be deducted from the deposit later.
- Exchange of contracts – Once you've paid the reservation fee, you'll usually have around 28 days to proceed to the exchange of contracts. Your solicitor will go through their regular conveyancing process, including local searches,

review of the contract, review of the draft lease agreement, etc. Once they're happy, you'll move on to the exchange of contracts. At this point, you'll pay the deposit, e.g. 10% of the agreed purchase price less the reservation fee, and you're legally committed to buying the property, once it's completed.

- Monitor the build progress – After exchange of contracts, you'll likely go pens down for a while, unless the off plan period is a short one. You should request regular updates from the developer and monitor the build progress. A few months before the development is due to complete, you'll need to start lining up your financing, so that it's ready and in place.

- Developer serves their 'notice to complete' – When the build is complete, the developer will serve you with a 'notice to complete', setting out the timeline for completion and giving you time to finalise your mortgage offer and satisfy the lender's valuation and other requirements.

- Completion of the purchase – Completion day is just like any other property purchase. You pay the rest of the purchase price across to the developer, and the property is yours. You'll want to make sure you pick up the keys yourself in person so that you can also take receipt of any documentation that comes with the property, e.g. NHBC warranties, electrical installation reports, fire safety reports, and any other paperwork passed on by the developer.

That's all there is to it, and apart from the reservation fee, the early exchange of contracts, and the off plan period, it's similar to any other property purchase.

The upsides of buying off plan

As a relatively hands-off investor myself, I like buying off plan, and I've done so a number of times. There are three key reasons investors choose to buy off plan.

The potential to get a good discount

With developers keen to make some early sales and get some money in the bank, there is always the potential for a discount, particularly if you're thinking about taking several units off their hands, either on your own or as part of a group. The level of discount you can achieve will depend somewhat on the attractiveness of the development and where we are in the property cycle, but you do want some kind of discount to compensate you for the risks involved, e.g. of the development not being completed and the fact your money is tied up over the off plan period. It's not uncommon to achieve discounts of between 5% and 15% below market value, depending on the development.

The property will be ready-to-let

Whether it's a new build or a residential conversion, the property should be ready to let out. Everything will either be new or refurbished, including the appliances, and the works will have been completed to modern standards. This means there should be less maintenance to worry about going forward, which can be perfect for hands-off investors. The property should also be more appealing from the tenant's perspective – it should be energy efficient, lowering their utility bills, and it should have that 'new property feel'. This can help your property stand out in the market for years to come, and it may help you secure a higher level of rent in the first few years, after the build is complete.

The benefits of extra leverage

With off plan deals, the deposit is often around 10% of the price. However, you will continue to be exposed to movements in property prices between exchange and completion. In a rising market, this extra leverage can boost your returns, but in a falling market this can be risky. Let's take a look at a simple example. Say you bought a one-bedroom apartment off plan for a purchase price of £100,000, and you put down a deposit of £10,000. If the project takes two years to complete and if property prices in the area rise by 4% p.a. over this period, the property will be worth £108,160 at completion. Your equity has grown by £8,160 compared with your money down of £10,000 – that's an ROI of 82% in two years. Of course, this extra leverage can also work against you in a falling market.

Keys to success

Buying property off plan is a slightly different investment proposition. There are some clear advantages for hands-off investors, but there are also some big risks that you'll need to manage. Here are some of the keys to success.

- Make sure your deposit is protected – Buying off plan, the biggest risk you face as an investor is that the developer goes bust and you lose your deposit. As such, you need to make sure that your deposit is properly protected and that the amount is low, preferably no higher than 10%. In practice, deposits are usually protected in one of two ways: (a) the money is placed in escrow, i.e. with a third party such as a solicitor, and the developer can't touch this until the build is complete; (b) the deposit is protected by an insurance-backed guarantee, such as that offered by NHBC's Buildmark Cover, which provides insurance protection, if you lose your deposit as a result of a builder becoming insolvent. Option (a) is rare, as most developers want access to the cash deposits; with Option (b), many insurance schemes pay out a maximum of 10% of the purchase price on insolvency, so, if your deposit is greater than 10%, it's likely some of this at risk. Try not to put down more than 10%.
- Research the developer's track record – You want to pick a developer with a strong track record and that you can have confidence in. Yes, it's great to have your deposit protected, but do you want the hassle of making an insurance claim? To combat this, make sure you research the developer to understand what projects they've delivered before and to make sure their financials look strong. For the medium to large developers, you can check their accounts on Companies House and do a Google search on their previous developments to see if you like what you see. For the smaller developers, you should research the directors of the business and see what you can find out about this company and any previous companies they've run.
- Don't neglect your due diligence – There's nothing inherently different about buying property off plan, it's a potential investment just like any other and it

should be treated as such. You should make sure you follow your regular due diligence process to verify the likely income and expenses for the property, speak to local agents about the prospects for the area and confirm the likely tenant demand, and build out the investment case for the property in the way you would for any other property. The deal should stand on its own two feet and compare favourably with alternative investments you might consider. This is no time to relax your criteria.

- Validate the level of discount – Occasionally when buying off plan, it can be difficult to assess the market value of the property and the level of discount you're getting. There may be no direct comparables, or harder still there may be no other blocks or properties in the area at all. In these situations, you need to work doubly hard to make sure the deal price is right and that you're getting a genuine discount. Your best bet here is to work off the sold prices of the closest available comparables, even if that is some way off. You should also speak to three or four local estate agents and see if they can help you pin down the market value. You might also consider asking the developer for sales data on other properties that have sold to date in the development – if nothing else, this data can help give you comfort that you're not overpaying relative to other buyers.

- Know what you're buying – Does the property come with white goods and appliances included? Will the flooring still need to be finished after you buy? Does the property come with a parking space, and, if so, are there any annual charges associated with this? What's the length of the lease, and does it allow you to sublet the property to tenants, either on a short or a long-term basis? Do you understand the plans and the pros and cons of the plot you're getting, including things like which floor it's on, proximity to the lifts, what the view will be like, and the level of natural light. When it comes to buying off plan, the devil is in the detail. You need to work hard to understand what you're buying and make sure you've fully factored this into your figures and the investment case for the property.

- Allow for uncertainty – When buying off plan, there will be less data available as part of your modelling. For one, the level of market rent will be unknown, as the property has never been let out before. In addition, you won't have access to two to three years of service charge and other data, meaning your costings will have some uncertainty attached, though the developer might be able to provide you with some kind of estimate here. As a result, you should be cautious in your modelling, and allow for some uncertainty.

- Check your contractual protections – There are some basic protections that you'll want to make sure are present in your contract when buying off plan. The first is a long-stop date. This is a date, usually set some time in the future, by which the developer needs to have completed the build. If the developer can't complete by this date, then you have the right (but not the obligation) to request your money back. The second is some kind of tolerance in the build specification, e.g. the floor space must be within 5% of the contract drawings. This is an area to speak to your solicitor about, as you'll want to make sure the contract provides you with sufficient protection in the event of a breach. If you can't get the legal protections you need, then don't do the deal.

- Know your mortgage options – Mortgage offers usually only last a maximum of six months. As such, the delay between exchange and completion means it's usually not possible to lock in your mortgage offer when you reserve your plot and exchange. This opens up the risk that at completion, you can't get the financing you need, because of a change in the mortgage market or your personal circumstances. To combat this risk, work with a good broker to help you find the right finance and the development itself is mortgageable before exchanging contracts. Ultimately, if you can't get a mortgage or if you can't get one on the terms you want, you might end up having to put more money into the deal or pull out of the purchase, risking your deposit.

- Avoid overheated markets – The extra leverage that comes with buying off plan can supercharge your returns in a rising market, but it can be risky in an overheated market. Suppose, for example, that prices fall by 20% before completion. In this case, you are still contractually committed to buying the property at the agreed price; however, your mortgage lender will be working off the new lower price. This means you might need to put more money into the deal or risk losing your deposit. To manage this risk, make sure you have enough of a cash buffer to deal with these types of situations, and try to avoid buying in an overheated market where prices could fall.

- Snag the property on completion – If you've not come across the term before, 'snagging' is the process of checking a new building for minor faults that need to be rectified. After completion, it's a good idea to use a snagging company to visit the property and catalogue all of the little things that you want the developer to fix. You'll want to do this as soon as possible after completion, while the developer is still on site, so they can attend to fixes quickly. If you don't pick up these problems up at the start, then you'll lose the opportunity, and you'll need to cover the costs yourself when your tenant spots problems three to six months later.

- Allow for an initial void period – Finally, you should be prepared for a void period immediately post-completion. With a glut of properties coming onto the rental market at the same time, it can be a bit of a lottery as to which ones rent out first and which ones rent out later. Depending on the area, the local market may take some time to absorb extra supply, so you can't guarantee you'll be able to let the property in the usual timeframes. To prepare for this, get a letting agent lined up, and start marketing the property as soon as you possibly can. One of the properties will be the first to let out, and you want it to be yours. This is only an issue when the development first completes, as the new tenancies will be different lengths, and the properties won't all come on to the market at the same time again.

These are just some of the keys to success when buying off plan. When it comes to buying off plan, research is really the key – you should think of this as doing all your normal due diligence plus a little bit more.

Reversal

Buying property off plan can be a great way to expand your portfolio. There's the opportunity for a discount, and the buying process can be simpler, with no chain to complicate things. However, there is one major drawback in that there's often no opportunity to add value. If you're a hands-on property investor with strong refurb skills and a strong network, or if you're relying on adding value to force an uplift in capital value and recycle your cash, then this approach is not a great fit for you and your strategy. If that sounds like you, you might be better off looking at one of the other BMV strategies detailed in these pages, if you're looking for a way to grow your portfolio faster that also uses your skills.

Play # 38 – The cash-only deal (BMV strategy # 5)

A few years into her property journey, Emily, a GP from Oxford, came into some money when her aunt passed away. Her previous deals were funded via personal savings, so the £275,000 inheritance was a game changer, opening up all kinds of possibilities. The strategy that appealed to her the most was the cash-only deal. She hoped that by pairing her newfound ability to drive a bargain in situations requiring a quick cash sale with periodic refinancing, she could fast track her investment progress.

When time is of the essence

This next play, which is all about cash-only deals, is the fifth and final of our BMV strategies. Buying a property in cash is not something every investor can do, and so these types of deals often carry a degree of intrigue and fascination. However, there's nothing inherently complicated or mysterious about them, just good old supply and demand playing itself out, with cash buyers using their ability to move quickly and to provide certainty in situations where you have a motivated seller that's under pressure to get a deal done quickly with a credible counterparty. In this play, we're going to look at what opportunities exist in this space, how doing a cash deal can be beneficial, and how to take advantage of the situation to get the best possible result. Every so often, an opportunity appears where a cash deal is not only possible, but hugely beneficial. When it does, you need to be ready to go.

An introduction to cash deals

The advantages of cash-only deals

Studies have found that buyers typically pay around 5% to 15% below market value when buying a property in cash. This means buying in cash can be a great way to secure a BMV deal and a great way to grow your portfolio. What's more, just because you bought the property in cash doesn't mean you can't use leverage to enhance your returns; after six months or a year, you can look to remortgage and pull out your cash for reinvestment. If you bought well and secured a BMV deal, it might be possible to remortgage at the property's true (uplifted) market value at the time, meaning you can leave even less of your own money in the deal. Of course, the longer the period of time before you remortgage, the greater your chances of success here, and it's not always possible to extract the maximum cash out of every refinance.

Even if you do remortgage later, there can be real benefits to buying in cash in the first place. Firstly, less people are able to buy in cash, so it makes your offer stand out. Secondly, your ability to transact quickly and to provide certainty that the transaction will go through can give the seller confidence that they're dealing with a credible counterparty. They can have confidence that a lender won't pull your financing and that there's no onward chain to disrupt or slow down the sale, and this can make you the preferred bidder and increase your chances of striking a deal, even in circumstances where you're offering less than the competition. Of course, speed and certainty are only a welcome currency for the most motivated sellers, which brings us on to the question of how to find cash deals.

How to find cash-only deals

Finding cash deals is all about finding a motivated seller who's willing to trade money in the bank for transaction speed and certainty. Ideally, you want to focus on deals where a cash transaction is not just a nice-to-have, but a necessity for the deal to go through in the first place, where the timescales involved prohibit doing the deal in any other way. There are two main ways to find cash deals:

1. Buying through an agent – One way to find cash deals is simply to approach estate agents in your target area and let them know you're a cash-buyer, that you're keen to do a deal, and that you can move quickly. Ask them if they have any properties on their books where the seller is looking for a quick sale and is prepared to accept a competitive offer. Approaching agents in this way might flush out some potential deals, like pre-repossessions, seller's keen on a quick sale for personal reasons, or perhaps even probate properties. More importantly, it will let the agent know they have an outlet for such deals in the future. You want them to look out for any deals that might be suitable for you in the future, so you want to come across as professional, dependable, and someone they can trust to get the deal through. This strategy is all about building long-term relationships and a personal network that delivers deals to your desk before they're even on the market. Make calls to the agents once a month to make sure you're front of mind.

2. Buying from developers – We touched on the types of deals and discounts available from developers in play # 37. However, there's also a chance to take advantage of cash deals with developers. Say, for example, a developer is at risk of not meeting their year-end sales targets, owing to a buyer pulling out of a deal or their financing falling through. In this situation, a developer may be keen to offload the units in question at a discounted price to a cash buyer capable of completing the purchase quickly and in time for their year-end. To take advantage of these deals, you need to make contact with the developer around six to eight weeks before their year-end, let them know you're keen to do a cash deal and that you can move quickly if opportunities arise, and then wait for their call. If you make regular contact throughout the period, there's a good chance you'll be contacted to do a deal. To put some process around this, make a list of national and regional builders you want to work with, along with their year-end dates, and get those calls in your diary.

How to make sure you're ready

With cash-only deals, it's all about your ability to move quickly, so you need to get yourself ready before you start putting your name and your reputation on the line. Here are my top three tips.

- Have a great solicitor in place – Having a great solicitor in place is crucial, and it can make the difference between a deal going through or not happening at all. Lining up a solicitor, preferably someone you've worked with before and had a good experience with, is important. Better still, you should work with someone you've got a strong existing relationship with that you can leverage when the pressure is on. A good solicitor will understand the criticality of the timeline and will work with you to solve problems, not create them.

- Make sure your funds are instantly accessible – If you're going to specialise in cash-only deals, then you need to make sure your funds are accessible at a moment's notice. Forget about locking up your funds in a term deposit for an extra 0.5% p.a. on the interest rate, the bigger prize here is the discount you can secure on the cash-only deal. Make sure your funds are kept in an account that can be accessed immediately, preferably the same day. I've seen deals go right to the wire, where investors haven't taken this step.

- Front-end load your research – In certain circumstances, it might be possible to front-end load your research, increasing your ability to act quickly. Say for example you're targeting deals from a local or regional developer in a specific area. In this case, it's no bad thing for you to research developments that are coming on line soon and get a feel for which ones are of interest, whether the deal financials work, and whether the fundamentals are there to make the investment case a strong one. If you know nothing about the development when a deal comes up, you're already on the back foot.

With all of that said, it's important not to lose sight of the big picture, despite the aggressive timeline and the fear of missing out. When you're under pressure and the stakes are high, it's easy to make poor decisions. Staying calm, in spite of all the pressure, is the name of the game. Sometimes that means turning down a deal where the timescales are unrealistic; sometimes that means paying attention to any last-minute changes to the terms or structure of the deal. If the deal changes in a way you're not happy with, don't do it. Lastly, it's worth stressing that you should not skip any fundamental due diligence, just to meet a tight deadline. You should still consider getting a survey and a valuation completed, despite there being no lender demanding this, and your solicitor still needs to go through the usual conveyancing process, including checks on the title, searches, and a review of any important legal documents.

Redux

Setting aside an opportunistic cash fund running into the hundreds of thousands of pounds is just not feasible for many investors. But there are ways to simulate this via other means. One option is to run with a smaller cash fund, say half of what you need based on your target deal size, and to develop alternative sources of funding that you can tap at short notice, via joint ventures, personal and family contacts, or even short-term bank loans secured against other collateral or assets you own. If you can pre-agree the terms of this lending before you need it, it will allow you to act quickly and meet the timescales typically needed to complete on cash deals. Another option is to go down the bridging finance route, securing the funds you need against the property itself or better still against an unencumbered property in your portfolio. Whilst this is likely to be slower than the first option, it may still be fast enough to give you the edge and allow you to take advantage of opportunities to transact on a cash basis. Whatever option you choose, make sure those additional costs from external financing are factored into your return calculations when assessing the viability of the deal and carefully consider your exit strategy, including the timeline for remortgaging. You should be upfront in all your dealings and clear with all parties on the timeline for repayment.

Play # 39 – Use the property cycle and ripple effect

Wendy and her husband Bob were landlords more than they were investors, preferring to self-manage and source properties in need of a refurb at their local auction house. Their portfolio was local to the area they lived, each one of their properties being within a 30-minute drive of their front door. This had worked well for years, while many of the local towns were on the up. But the local market was hot right now, and deals were no longer providing good cash flow. Did they need to change their approach?

Surfing the property wave

This play is all about how to use the property cycle to build your portfolio over the medium to long term. The property cycle itself is perhaps one of the most misused ideas in property investment. Many people have heard of the cycle, but lots of the discussions around it are either overly simplistic or overly definitive. Many pundits use the cycle predictively to express grand views about how the property market will play out in the future. This often includes giving down-to-the-year style crystal ball predictions about when the market will peak and when it will crash, which in my view is just not possible for markets as complex as the housing market or economic systems in general, for that matter. I'm going to try to set the record straight a little and give you my views on what's possible as far as predicting the future goes. Hopefully it will provide some balance.

Once we've run through the basics of the property cycle, what it is and why it happens, we'll look at some rules you can follow when growing your portfolio to take advantage of the cycle. We'll also talk about how you can position yourself at various points in the cycle to increase your chances of success and minimise your downside risk. The best you can really hope for is to tip the odds in your favour, as no-one really knows how the future will play out. However, being able to spot the general trends and avoid expensive mistakes can, over the long term, have a big impact on your success as a property investor. That's what this play is really all about.

What is the property cycle?

The property cycle is a sequence of recurrent events, a pattern if you will, that plays out across different property markets. Like other investments, property tends to follow a fairly predictable cycle. The cycle itself has four different phases. I'm going to walk you through each of these phases with a commentary on what typically happens at each stage in the cycle.

The recovery phase

Let's start out with the recovery phase. At the beginning of this phase, prices have just fallen in a recent market crash. Prices have in fact fallen to a level where yields are strong and monthly cash flows are good. This is because prices have fallen more than rents. For contrarian investors with cash resources to spare, this is a fantastic time to be buying property.

At this point in the cycle, there will be few active buyers in the market. The average investor will have been badly burned in the crash and is still licking their wounds. They may have sold at the bottom of the market and crystallised large losses. The media will be downbeat, even though the worst of the recession appears to be over and property prices have stabilised somewhat.

As rents and cash flows start to increase, and as brave investors lend support to prices, the recovery phase starts to develop. More and more buyers acquire the confidence to re-enter the market. Property prices start to rise. This happens in the prime locations first, with early price growth being mainly in the big cities and city centre hotspots. Then it starts to ripple out.

The boom phase

With the recovery gathering pace, the market will move into the explosive boom phase. At the start of the boom, it will now be clear that prices are increasing. More investors will be returning to the market. The banks will have repaired their balance sheets, and they are now keen to lend again. This will provide a boost to the market, as cheap-and-easy financing increases.

House prices start to increase at a faster pace. Prime cities and city centre locations will switch into another gear and unloved secondary locations will start to see their first price rises. Better times and an improved economic backdrop will make providers of capital more optimistic. Banks will start to forget the lessons of the last crash, as financing becomes easier still.

Now we're well into the boom phase. Yields have fallen and higher property prices have made cash flows less strong, except perhaps in secondary locations. Savvy investors are struggling to make property deals work. They can't find value anywhere, so they stop striking deals. They might even sell a property or two to lock-in their gains, but no-one will pay attention. The public, encouraged by the recent price rises, begin to speculate on property investments. Property shows are all over the airwaves.

The mania phase

At a certain point, logic appears to leave the market and groupthink takes over. We're now entering the mania phase. Banks have relaxed their lending criteria as far as they can go, and credit standards are what can only be described as lax. The higher prices go, the more everyone believes they will continue to do so. The vast amount of money pouring into the market keeps prices going up and up. We're now into the last couple of years of the explosive boom phase. This is often called the "winner's curse" – if you're the last person to buy at the peak of the market, you're the one who will take the hit in the crash, which is just around the corner.

The crash or slump phase

Just before the crash, the market is driven purely by sentiment, not fundamentals. At some point, confidence starts to dip a little. The banks begin to look at their ballooning loan books and worry about whether some of these loans will ever be repaid. Financing suddenly dries up, almost overnight it seems, and confidence evaporates completely, taking the market with it.

Property prices plummet. Individuals and investors who are over-leveraged will go bankrupt. This triggers a wave of repossessions and forced property sales which add to the downward pressure on prices. The media stokes the fire with bad news headlines. And speculators who bought at the peak and are in negative cash flow positions sell up, crystallising their losses.

After a year or two of falling prices and bad economic data, we start to see the first green shoots of recovery. Unemployment peaks and rents stop falling. Brave investors start to look at deals again. To their surprise, some of these deals start to look attractive. If only they could raise the capital to invest. The odd bank agrees to start lending again, albeit the financing terms are tougher. Investors are asked to put in 40% or more of the purchase price themselves, that is a 60% LTV mortgage. The recovery phase gets underway, and the cycle starts again.

The length of a typical cycle

In the narrative above, I've described how elements such as investor psychology, attitudes to risk and availability of financing feed into the property cycle. These are elements most financial cycles have in common, including the property cycle. But the property cycle incorporates one other element that other financial cycles don't share, and that's long lead times.

In the property market, there can be significant lead times before buildings come on to the market to meet additional demand. Developers need to carry out economic feasibility studies. They need to find and purchase a new piece of land or development site. The building has to be designed, planning permissions have to be granted, and financing has to be secured. And all this needs to take place before developers can put a spade in the ground and start construction. All in all, the property development process can take years. For a major project, the whole process can take more than a decade from start to finish.

Long lead times in the development process are then a major driver on the supply side and influence the length of a typical property cycle. Property cycles can last anywhere between 15 and 25 years from peak to peak or from crash to crash, and the cycle can interact with other cycles in the wider economy.

The important thing to remember is that property prices generally increase in line with inflation or higher over the long term. But the cycle means these price increases don't happen in a linear fashion. Prices will increase faster in the boom phase, and they will fall or stagnate in the crash or slump phase. But the overall trend is generally upwards and in line with inflation.

Spotting where we are in the cycle

We can get some clues on where we are in the cycle by looking at the things going on around us. For example, in the recovery, we'll have recently experienced a fall in prices and property will be out-of-favour. Plenty of people will be in negative equity, and the press headlines will be downbeat. Financing will be hard to get, and building projects started in the boom will be left unfinished. The odd brave developer might take on one of these projects as a repossession, and as activity starts to pick up, prices start to rise a little.

In the boom phase, lenders will be lending, and builders will now be building. People will have forgotten the pain of the last crash and property will attract headlines as prices start to soar. Lots of new building projects will be started and cranes will fill the skyline. In the final years of a boom, the media will be blurting out all kinds of nonsense. Financing will be cheap, and massive vanity projects like huge skyscrapers will be announced. Prices will make no sense. It will feel like a bubble, because it is one. Then comes the crash or slump. No description is needed. Trust me, you'll know when you're in a crash.

How to use the property cycle

To finish off this chapter, I'm going to look at how you can use the property cycle to grow your portfolio. I'm going to give you my five golden rules of portfolio building. Some of these are straightforward; however, one of the hardest things to do over the long term is to keep your investment focus crystal clear and to keep your head when others around you are losing theirs. I hope you will keep these golden rules in mind over the years.

Golden rule # 1 – Only invest in properties that provide cash flow

This really is the most important rule of property investing. If a property doesn't provide you with a monthly cash, preferably one with a good margin for safety, then you shouldn't be doing the deal in the first place.

When it comes to the property cycle, the best time to be buying from a cash flow perspective is in the recovery phase and at the start of the boom. Later on in the cycle, yields will have fallen, and cash flow will be hard to find. That doesn't mean you shouldn't be investing at all later in the cycle, but it does mean you'll likely have a much harder time striking good deals.

If you follow this rule diligently, it'll mean being more aggressive and ramping up your investing activities when cash flows are at their strongest in the early part of the cycle. It'll also mean refraining from bad deals later in the cycle.

Golden rule # 2 – Use the ripple effect to your advantage

Predicting which areas and which properties will experience good capital growth in the future is a really difficult thing to do. The best tool in the property investor's tool kit is to try to take advantage of the ripple effect in some way.

As we saw in the descriptions above, different towns and cities experience growth at different points in the cycle. Let's take the 2007-2008 financial crisis for instance. After falling to a low in 2009, property prices rebounded in London. First, we saw growth in the prime areas of central London, then price increases rippled out to the surrounding areas. It took several years before prices in Leeds started to rise. Between 2014 and 2018, however, prime properties in the city centre of Leeds experienced strong growth, but properties on the outskirts of town have yet to experience the same level of growth.

Let's try to generalise this rule slightly. Early in the cycle, properties in prime cities and prime locations will likely experience the first bout of capital growth. This growth will start to make properties slightly further out look comparatively cheaper, and so this price growth will ripple out. To take advantage of the ripple effect, you need to buy in the right location at the right time. You'll need to study how prices are increasing in different towns and cities at various points in the cycle and try to get in ahead of the trend. Another way to use the ripple effect is to invest in areas which are set to receive big investment. This could, for example, mean investing in areas close to city centre regeneration projects or near to big infrastructure projects like HS2 that will improve transport links.

Golden rule # 3 – Manage your leverage carefully

If you've bought well during the recovery phase and used the ripple effect to your advantage, you may well have experienced strong capital growth by the later part of the cycle. At this point, you might be tempted to remortgage one or more of your properties and pull out some of your capital to expand your portfolio. If you do decide to do this, make sure you model the impact on cash flows (see Golden rule # 1). The increase in borrowing will increase your finance costs and reduce your cash flow (we discussed this in play # 32). So, you should do this only if the property has experienced an increase in market rent and cash flows.

Some investors, I'm one of them, like to keep an unencumbered property or two in their portfolio. Having properties with no mortgage means you'll have a stronger monthly cash flow to ride out any dip in market rents or an increase in interest rates. You'll also have a strategic asset you can sell or mortgage, if you suddenly need to find a chunk of cash quickly. Being over-leveraged is the biggest risk for property investors, so make sure you manage this risk carefully.

Golden rule # 4 – Avoid the winner's curse

The last couple of years of the boom period are the winner's curse – avoid it like the plague. In short,, don't buy any new properties and don't refinance. Use this time to get ready for the crash that's coming.

Golden rule # 5 – Build a tactical cash buffer before the slump

We've all heard the Warren Buffett quote "we simply attempt to be fearful when others are greedy and to be greedy only when others are fearful". Well, Golden Rule # 4 covers the first part, but what about the second bit of this mantra?

To take advantage of a crash or slump, you'll need to build up your resources during the boom phase to take advantage of the crash. You should aim to build as big a cash buffer as you can in the years before the slump. If you've stopped doing deals and your cash flows are strong, then this should be achievable. Likewise, if you've kept a couple of properties unencumbered, there could be some creative things you can do on the financing side to secure the lending you need, at the right time. For example, you could allow a lender to take a first mortgage charge on an unencumbered property.

Finally, managing your emotions will also be key here. You'll feel like you're missing out on the end of the boom phase and that you could be putting that spare cash to much better use, but don't. Stay disciplined, and you'll be thankful later. Controlling your emotions and sticking to your principles is actually the hardest part about investing for many people, so don't overlook this point. Investing with a partner and making decisions together can help here, as can coming up with a set of financial metrics or decision-making rules that define when you will and won't invest. Don't be tempted to flex these rules without a good reason.

Play # 40 – Churning your portfolio over time

Eloise started investing in property in her early thirties, and she'd done well for herself, building a portfolio of twelve buy-to-lets over fifteen years. Her portfolio was making strong profits of around £3,000 per month, but she still had further to go to reach her goals, and she wasn't keen to put more money in herself – now was the time to buy that dream house she wanted. For Eloise, the next phase of her journey was all about managing her assets, picking out the best properties she could find and repositioning for growth.

A coming-of-age story

If you stick with property over the long term, there will come a time when enough is enough, when the properties in your portfolio are sufficient to meet your goals and when you don't want or need to accumulate any more. At this point, the focus shifts, as you move from the accumulation phase to the long-term management phase, and it becomes sensible to 'churn' your property portfolio every year or every couple of years to improve quality. You can do this by selling any properties that are underperforming, refinancing where growth has been strong, and better positioning your portfolio for future growth. You might also decide it's time to take some risk off the table by reducing your mortgage debt or that you'd like to manage fewer properties and free up some of your time. We'll take a look at all this and more right here in play # 40.

Why churn your portfolio?

There's only one thing certain in property and life, and that's change. Even if you invested in the best deals available and positioned your portfolio well for future growth, fast forward a few years, and it's unlikely those same properties would still be the best possible capital allocation. As such, it makes sense to review your portfolio from time to time and see what you can do to improve it. For me, there are three principal aims of churning your portfolio:

1. To drive an increase in profitability – Not all of the properties you've invested in will be great, especially those early deals. It makes financial sense to weed out the less good investments and put that money to better use. Over time, this can help you drive some big increases in profitability.

2. To reposition your portfolio for growth – We learned all about the property cycle and the ripple effect in our last play. Using the market cycle to manage your portfolio means moving out of areas that have seen some high growth (and which are unlikely to experience similar levels of growth in the future) and moving into areas and locations where the growth is yet to come.

3. To reduce your management time – Occasionally, in the course of investing, you'll pick up a property that just seems to attract problems. Sometimes it's a property that's prone to repairs and needs round-the-clock maintenance; sometimes it's a property that seems to attract difficult tenants. You can use this opportunity to identify and offload 'problem properties' like this.

Lastly, it's worth saying there are lots of other reasons you might choose to sell properties from time-to-time. One of the main ones is to reduce the leverage in your portfolio, e.g. by selling a property that's experienced strong capital growth and using the proceeds to pay down your remaining mortgage balances. This can help investors to reduce their exposure to interest rate risk, and it's something many investors choose to do as their portfolio grows in size. If you're looking for more on this, I cover portfolio risk management techniques in detail in Chapter 9 of my first book, *Essential Property Investment Calculations*.

Another reason to sell properties is if you've had a change in circumstances or strategy. Say, for example, you're approaching retirement and you're about to give up the day job. Your goals might switch more towards income generation, and you might decide to sell any lower yielding properties that have experienced strong capital growth and reinvest the funds in higher yielding properties which generate a greater monthly cash flow. These are all valid reasons for churning your portfolio, and you should factor these other aims and objectives into your decision making as well.

A simple mental model

Next, we're going to take a look at a simple model for churning your portfolio over time. It's a simple two-by-two matrix (the type consultants love) you can apply to each property in your portfolio. Let's take a look at how it works.

		Low cap rate	High cap rate
Capital growth	High growth	Take your gains (sell the property)	Recycle your cash (remortgage)
	Low growth	Cut your losses (sell the property)	Hold your ground (do nothing)
		Capitalisation rate	

The model asks you to look at each of the properties in your portfolio from two different lenses: (1) the first lens, along the bottom, is the current capitalisation rate, based on the current market value of the property; (2) the second lens, up the side, is the capital growth experienced by the property since you bought it or since it was last remortgaged. Let's take a walk round the four quadrants and see what types of properties might fall into those buckets and what the best action to take is at each point.

Take your gains (top left quadrant)

In the top left corner are properties which have experienced good growth since you bought them or since they were last remortgaged. The capitalisation rate is low, as rents haven't increased at the same pace as property prices, and it's not possible to remortgage and increase your leverage without hurting your ROI and pushing the property into a much worse cash flow position. In this case, your best move financially is to sell up, take your gains, and reinvest the equity released in higher yielding properties that have better growth potential. The only time you should hang on to the property is if you have a conviction that property prices will increase faster here than elsewhere, or if you think rents are likely to bounce back, unlocking the potential for remortgaging further down the line.

Recycle your cash (top right quadrant)

In the top right corner are properties that have experienced high growth, but where the capitalisation rate is still high. In this case, you've been fortunate that rents have grown in line with property prices, and it's possible to remortgage and increase your leverage without hurting your ROI. The higher borrowing will, of course, reduce your cash flow, but probably not enough to push you into a cash flow negative position. And as long as the ROI on your new investment is greater than the cost of borrowing, you'll have improved the cash flow for your portfolio overall. In this case, your best move financially is to go ahead with the remortgage and recycle that cash into new investments. The only time I would advise against this option is if it's late in the property cycle and you expect the market could be vulnerable to prices and rents falling in the near future.

Hold your ground (bottom right quadrant)

In the bottom right corner are properties that have experienced no or low levels of capital growth since you bought them or since they were last remortgaged. For these properties, the capitalisation rate is still high, meaning that you're making a decent return on your capital, and so there's no immediate need to do anything. In fact, the high cap rate may be an indicator that there's still room for the price of the property to grow, so it could be a sign of growth to come. However, there's not been enough growth for you to consider remortgaging the property. For now, your best bet is to sit tight, hold your ground, and manage the property as best you can to keep those returns coming.

Cut your losses (bottom left quadrant}

In the bottom left corner are properties that have experienced no or low levels of capital growth, but where the capitalisation rate is low. Rental profits will be poor for these properties, owing to either a fall in market rents or higher than expected rental costs. If the property is cash flow positive, then you might choose to hang onto it and wait for an opportune time to sell, for example, in the later stages of the property cycle. In the worst cases, the property may have turned cash flow negative, in which case your best financial move might be to sell up right away and reinvest that capital elsewhere. If property prices have fallen, and if selling would crystallise that loss, you could inject some capital to reduce your leverage, increase your cash flow, and wait until prices have recovered. There are no easy options with properties in this quadrant, but you can try your best to follow what the figures are telling you and to take your emotions out of the situation.

The cut-off points

So far, we've talked quite generally about what to do with each of these property types, but is it possible to be more specific about the quantitative measures that you might use to help you decide which quadrant the property actually falls into? For example, what's the boundary between properties with a high cap rate and a low cap rate? Where's the dividing line between properties that have experienced low capital growth and high capital growth? Let's take a look at each of these cut-off points in turn and how to decide which properties fall where.

With capitalisation rate, r_c, it's all about how that rate compares with the cost of borrowing, r_b. The capitalisation rate, r_c, tells us how much profit you make for each pound of money (your money or the lender's money) that's invested in the property. Likewise, the borrowing rate, r_b, tells us how much it costs for each pound of money borrowed from the lender. If the capitalisation rate, r_c, is bigger than our borrowing rate, r_b (that is, if $r_c > r_b$) then it makes sense to borrow money and invest it in the property, as the return generated on the borrowed funds is greater than the borrowing cost. In this case, we'll increase our ROI by using leverage. However, if the capitalisation rate, r_c, is less than our borrowing rate, r_b (that is, if $r_c < r_b$) then it does not make sense to borrow money and invest it in the property, as the return generated on the borrowed funds is less than the cost of borrowing. In this case, we'll decrease our ROI by using leverage. As such, in the diagram a few pages back, properties with a 'high' capitalisation rate and which fall on the right-hand side of the diagram are those with a cap rate that's a decent amount higher (at least 0.5% to 1.0% higher) than the borrowing rate. Properties with a 'low' capitalisation rate and which fall on the left-hand side of the diagram are those with a cap rate that's close to or less than the borrowing rate. In practice, the cost of borrowing varies for each individual and can also vary between different types of investment. This means the boundary may be different for each property in your portfolio.

With capital growth, it's all about choosing a cut-off point that strikes the right balance between efficiency and expense. If you choose a low cut-off point, which means you'll be selling and remortgaging frequently, there will be a high level of expenses associated with this. If you choose a high cut-off point, which means you'll be selling and remortgaging infrequently, you might be leaving your capital tied up in underperforming properties for longer or expanding your portfolio less quickly than you otherwise might, leading to less optimal returns. In practice, the best strategy is likely to be one that aims to minimise transaction expenses, but which looks to recycle your capital into new, profitable investments as soon as there's been a meaningful gain. A practical cut-off point for most investors would be capital growth of around 10%. Below the 10% level, the expenses associated with the sale or remortgage are likely to eat up much of the gain from the exercise. Above the 10% level, the exercise will be much more worthwhile. Again, this cut-off will vary depending on the type of properties you're investing in and their market values. So, make sure you think this through carefully for each property, and, as we discussed in play # 32, make sure you watch out for early repayment charges which could increase the cost of a potential sale or remortgage.

Keys to success

Churning your portfolio over time is something you'll need to get good at to take your property investing to the next level. There are big rewards on offer for those who get it right, but there are also some big risks you'll need to manage. Here are some of the keys to success with this exercise.

- Use numbers to guide your decision making – Any decision you make should be based on an analysis of the numbers. You should look at the net profit and capitalisation rate you're making for each property, rather than basing your decision on gut feel. If you're unclear how to do the mathematics needed to assess the historical performance, take a look at Chapter 7 of my first book, *Essential Property Investment Calculations*, for a set-by-step guide.
- Take a long-term view – When you're deciding which properties to sell and which to keep, make sure you take a long-term view of their performance. It doesn't usually take long to spot a complete dud, but equally you don't want to sell a good property because of one bad year, where expenses have been higher than normal. When you're assessing a property's capitalisation rate, make sure you use a long-term average, over say three to five years.
- Make use of your tax allowances – When selling an investment property, any gains you make will be subject to taxation. If you're investing in your own

name or with a spouse, you should spread your sales out over time to make the best use of your capital gains tax (CGT) allowances, which you can offset against the capital gain you make to lower your tax bill. You can find details on the gov.uk website. If you're investing through a limited company, then any gain you make will be taxed at corporation tax rates.

- Use the property cycle to your advantage – In the later stages of the property cycle, the mania phase in particular, there will be lots of hype about property and even underperforming properties will likely be sat on some decent gains. You can use this as an opportunity to offload one or more underperforming properties, either to reinvest the proceeds elsewhere or potentially to build an opportunistic cash buffer in advance of the crash or slump.

- Avoid the sunk cost fallacy – Many investors hang on to underperforming investments far longer than they should. Some investors are reluctant to cut their losses, owing to the pain of admitting they've made a bad investment, the effort they've put into a deal, or potentially a fondness for the property in question, e.g. if it's one they've lived in themselves at a point in time. Try to approach these decisions objectively and avoid the sunk cost fallacy.

Reversal

There's an unwritten rule in property that says you should never sell a property. Whilst I don't agree with this rule, for all the reasons outlined, it's worth taking a moment to explore the rationale. The logic for this supposition is three-fold: (1) selling a property will incur costs, like taxes, legal fees and voids; (2) it's difficult to time the market, and once you've sold a property that money will be out of the market and you may miss out on some gains; (3) it's also difficult to predict the next hotspot, and you might sell up just before an area goes through a period of strong capital growth. In my view, there is merit to some of these arguments, and you may aim to keep the churn of your portfolio to a low level because of this. Being more active with these decisions brings more risk, and it needs to be a level of risk you're comfortable with.

Part Five : Advanced investment techniques

Play # 41 – Trading properties for a profit

Colin was a prolific property trader who loved the thrill of the chase. On his own patch, Colin knew the price of everything, right down to the street – pals in his property circle actually called him 'Rightmove'. Over a ten-year period, Colin had built an enviable position with local agents; he traded in cash and was trusted to complete deals quickly and in good faith. Local agents came to him with off-market deals and potential trading opportunities. It was a network that made him tens of thousands of pounds in income each year.

Buying property to sell

Trading properties for a profit is the next strategy on our list, and it's the first of ten advanced property investment techniques that we'll cover. Although it's not property investment per se, trading properties can be a fantastic way to make chunks of cash quickly, which you can use to finance future projects. It's not an easy thing to do, and it relies on being able to find trading opportunities, become laser-focussed on the numbers, and execute each step in the buying and selling process to perfection. In this play, I'm going to give you a crash course in how to trade properties. We're going to look at how the strategy works, where you can find properties to trade, and at some keys to success. It's a play few property investors actually utilise, owing to the unique skills and mindset required to be successful, but it's one that can be a game changer.

How does it work

Trading properties for a profit is a simple concept. It involves buying a property at one price, then quickly selling at a higher price. The big difference between this and flipping properties for a profit, which we covered in play # 25, is that with property trading, we're not looking to "add value" through refurbishment; we're simply trying to buy a property below market value and make a profit by selling at its true market value.

With property trading, it's fine to engage in basic cleaning and in the staging and presentation of the property, which we'll come back to later. You might even consider any quick and cheap fixes, as well as simple cosmetic changes like a coat of paint and making sure everything is in good working order, but any more than that and you're into refurb territory. The aim of the game is to turn the property around quickly and to get it sold fast as you can, so you should only be considering small changes that will take a week or two at most.

Working out the numbers

The mathematics behind property trading is simple. The profit formula is just like that for any other retail business.

$$Profit = Sale\ price - Purchase\ price - Costs$$

Say, for example, we managed to buy an apartment at auction for £130,000, and we sell it through an estate agent a month later for £165,000, with our transaction costs being around £11,000 in total. In this case, our trading profit before tax would be £165,000 – £130,000 – £11,000 = £24,000.

Another useful calculation is the potential return on investment for any trades you're considering. To see what the example above gives us as an ROI, we simply take our trading profit of £24,000 ÷ £141,000 (i.e. the money we've put into the deal, including the purchase price of £130,000 and our trading costs of £11,000) which is an ROI of 17% before tax. That's not bad for a month's work.

Finally, it's worth fleshing out the types of transaction costs that you'll need to cover with this strategy. On the buy-side, you'll need to cover the cost of stamp duty, as well as any professional fees like legal expenses and the cost of a survey. In addition, if you buy at auction, you'll also need to cover the auctioneer's fee. On the sell-side, you'll need to cover the estate agent's fee for selling the property, as well as a second set of legal expenses dealing with the sale. In the middle, you'll need to cover any costs relating to cleaning and cosmetic fixes that you carry out, as well as some small additional costs for the holding period, including insurance, utility bills and council tax. These costs won't be huge, but they need accounting for, nonetheless. I've set out below a breakdown of the £11,000 of costs incurred, split between buying, selling and holding costs.

Purchase costs

Stamp duty	£4,000
Auctioneer's fee (1% of purchase price)	£1,300
Legal expenses	£1,200
Building survey	£500
Total purchase costs	£7,000

Holding costs

Insurance	£50
Utility bills and council tax	£200
Cleaning, small fixes, painting	£750
Total holding costs	£1,000

Selling costs

Estate agent's fee	£1,650
Legal expenses	£1350
Total selling costs	£3,000

Total transaction costs	£11,000

Picking the ideal property

Finding a suitably trading opportunity and securing the deal at the right price is never going to be easy. Before we get into the specifics of where and how you can find properties to trade, we're going to discuss the three factors that all need to be present in order to create a great trading opportunity.

- The right area – The property needs to be located in an area where the local market is buoyant. That's because you'll want to sell as quickly as possible, once the property ready and available. In addition, you should pick an area that's popular with owner-occupiers, not investors. Family neighbourhoods with good local schools and strong transport links are ideal. Make sure you research any target areas thoroughly before you proceed.

- The right property – The best properties to trade are ones which will appeal to the largest number of buyers. The more buyers there are, the quicker you'll be able to sell and the greater the chances you'll find two competing buyers to push up the final sale price. Three-bedroom detached and semi-detached properties are ideal, as they will appeal to many different types of buyer. Bungalows can also work well for retirees.

- The right situation – The last leg of our tripod is the right situation. You need to buy property below market value, so the vendor needs to be a motivated seller looking for a quick sale or someone who's willing to give you a discount for some other reason. We'll look at some specific situations where deals are possible below, but it's safe to say that in general these opportunities arise from doing something different or seeing an angle others have missed.

The cardinal sin of property trading has to be buying what looks like a great value property in a remote, low-demand location. This is one of the hardest mistakes to rectify, as you won't be able to conjure up that demand yourself, no matter how good your marketing. As with all other aspects of property investment, the key again is research – above all else, make sure that the end demand is there.

Where to find properties to trade

Trading properties for a profit necessitates buying property below market value. We've looked at a number of ways to buy BMV in earlier chapters, and many of these can be used to generate trading opportunities too. In the list below, I've set out the main ways that traders use to find deals and generate opportunities.

- Auctions – With auction properties typically selling between 15% and 35% below market value, auctions are great place to find deals. You're looking for something you could tidy up with minimal effort and quickly sell on through an estate agent. Mismatched properties, e.g. a property in Sheffield selling at an auction house in Bournemouth, can be good buying opportunities, as you may be able to secure a much better price through a local agent or auction.

- Tenanted property – It's difficult for landlords and investors selling tenanted property to secure top dollar, as access can be difficult and potential buyers can struggle to see past the messiness tenants create. If you can see past this and think of a way to stage the property to have maximum impact and appeal to owner-occupiers, you might be able to create a trading opportunity.

- Direct search – Traders often focus on a local market they know really well. For these types of property traders, direct search – that is, finding properties that look empty or in need of a makeover – can be a great way to find trading opportunities. Simply contact the owner and make them an offer.

- Direct mail and local marketing – Direct outreach through leaflet campaigns and ads in local newspapers can generate off-market buying opportunities. You should look for motivated sellers in need of a quick sale. Try to reach an agreement with them before they list the property with a local agent.

- Your property network – Someone in your network of contacts, be that other property investors, estate agents, or tradespeople, might have spotted a deal that doesn't work for them or that they don't have capacity to take on. Having a network of contacts that come to you with potential opportunities is a great asset, and it can reap rewards, if you're willing to put in the upfront effort.

- Off plan property – We've discussed buying off plan at length in play # 37, so I won't cover that again. However, if you're buying in bulk or early on in the development process, buying off plan can be a great way to secure a discount and can be a trading opportunity, e.g. by selling shortly after completion. You need to be careful, as the leverage aspect can work for you or against you, and you could be nursing large losses if the market moves against you in the off plan period. If you're buying multiple units, you need to be extra careful around the risks of not being able to raise finance.

- Breaking up a portfolio – Finally, there's a trading strategy for investors with a little bit more cash at their disposal that involves buying a whole portfolio from another investor, say of five to ten properties or more, and selling the properties one by one with an estate agent. In this case, the profit comes from the fact that you will buy the whole portfolio at a discount to the sum of the market values of the individual properties, e.g. at a purchase price that's 15% to 25% below what the properties are worth individually.

None of these are easy. Finding a suitable property and buying it at the right price is hard, so it's going to take a lot of upfront effort, a refined, systematic approach, and strong negotiation skills to see any meaningful results.

Keys to success

To get this strategy right, you'll need to treat this endeavour as a business in its own right, putting in the time and energy it needs to succeed. Here are just some of the keys to success, if you want to become a profitable property trader:

- Tax treatment – If your trading activity is carried out via a limited company, the company will pay corporation tax on its trading profits at the end of its financial year. If you trade properties in your own name, your trading profits will be taxed under the income tax regime for individuals. Make sure you understand the tax rules and get set up with the right tax structure.

- Financing your flip – Most successful property traders execute their trades as cash deals. That's because buying in cash allows you to move quickly and seize opportunities when they arise. You could use bridging finance, but the arrangement and broker fees involved will eat into your trading profits.

- Getting the numbers right – When you're running your numbers, be prudent with your estimates and do enough research that you can be confident in the final sale price. Most traders aim for an ROI in the range 15% to 20%. That way, even if the sale price achieved is 10% lower than their estimate, they should still be able to breakeven or even squeeze out a small profit.

- Stage the property – Staging the property, that is, using furniture and props to tell potential buyers a visual story about how they will use the property, can make a big difference in converting viewings into offers, generating that competition and pushing up the final sale price. If you're trading properties regularly, you can keep your own stock of furniture and buy a van to help you move this around from one property to the next.

- Pick a good agent – When picking an estate agent, you want to use an agent that's active and which appeals to the type of buyer you're looking to attract. Carry out desktop research, using the portals like Rightmove and Zoopla to understand which agents are active and which have the best sales records. Also, make sure you understand their fees and cost these into your model.

- Pricing the property – When it comes to pricing the property, you'll want to pitch it at a low enough level to generate interest, but at a high enough level that you could make some concessions and still secure your desired profit. Speak to your agent to get their advice on this, and make sure the property is priced competitively enough to stand out versus others in the market.

- Keep your trading costs low – As we saw in the example above, trading costs can run into thousands of pounds, so it's important to keep these as low as you can. In practice, this means trading in cash, avoiding bridging finance, shopping for the best quote with solicitors, and potentially doing away with a survey, if the property is in great condition or has been built recently. If you live locally or have local contacts to help out with viewings, you could also consider selling the property yourself using one of the services that allow you to list your property on the portals like Rightmove and Zoopla yourself. This can be a great way to reduce your selling costs.

- Force it through – Remember that one third of property sales in England and Wales fall through after having an offer accepted, so you need to make sure you're actively chasing solicitors and agents every few days for an update to push the sale through. Any delays will eat into your profits through increased holding costs.

- Have a back-up plan – It's never a good idea to get into a trade expecting it to fail, but blind optimism won't help here either. As such, you should make sure you develop a back-up plan, in case you can't sell at your desired price. That plan could involve selling for an acceptable loss after a certain period of time, letting the property out to a tenant and refinancing onto a mortgage product, or simply wait it out, if you think it's a temporary dip in the market.

As a final word of caution, one of the biggest risks you face as a trader is that the overall market takes a nosedive. Because of that, you should avoid local markets that are overheated and abstain from trading in the latter stages of the property cycle. As with any other trading activity, make sure you understand the risks and that you're convinced the upside outweighs the downside. If it's possible, in the worst-case scenario, that you might lose 10% or 20% of your money, make sure you can live with this. Trading is as much a battle of emotions as it is a battle of wits, and mastery of your emotions is a key skill all traders need to develop.

Play # 42 – Investing for income with HMOs

Aldo needed a strategy that gave him the largest possible ROI, as he wanted to reach financial independence quickly. He'd always dreamed of running his own business, and he saw HMOs as an approach that could allow him to do that. His aim was to quit his job, go into property full time, and be his own boss within three years. With his savings pot of £240,000, all he needed was three large HMOs each generating an ROI of 15% per year, and he'd be able to generate the £3,000 per month he needed to support his wife and family. If his wife kept her job too, they'd even be able to afford a few holidays.

Taking buy-to-let to the next level

What if I told you there was a property strategy that generates high cash flow and which could allow you to replace the income from your job in a short timeframe? Yes, it requires lots of work, but you'd be your own boss. Depending on how much you like your job, you might find this proposition appealing. That's what our next play, investing in HMOs, is all about. It's a strategy many newcomers to property get pretty excited about, as it offers big headline returns and can make a big difference to your finances in a short space of time. In this chapter, we're going look at some of the pros and cons of HMO investments, take a run through a real-life worked example, and give you some top tips on how to run a successful HMO and avoid the common pitfalls and mistakes.

An introduction to HMOs

It's many investor's dream to buy a small number of properties that generate a large amount of rental income, and HMOs are a strategy that will let you do that. I know you're eager to get into all the juicy detail, but first things first – let's define what a HMO actually is and look at the different types of HMO you could run.

What is a HMO?

A 'house in multiple occupation', or HMO for short, is a home made up of *three or more people* who form *more than one household* – in short, three or more people living together that aren't all from the same family. HMOs are a type of multi-let, and they can generate higher rental income than single lets, owing to the fact the overall level of rent charged is determined on a room-by-room basis. However, they also require more management and come with higher running costs.

Types of HMO

HMOs are typically located in and around city centres. There are two main types of HMO that investors usually consider setting up, based on the type of market they're trying to serve. These are as follows:

1. Student HMOs – This type of HMO is set up to serve students, typically those studying at one of the large universities. The student HMO market has its own characteristics, e.g. a predictable lettings cycle based on the academic year, tenants contracting jointly on a single shared (AST) tenancy agreement, and an eleven-month letting year, amongst other things.
2. Professional HMOs – This type of HMO is set up to serve young professionals, and so they're usually located in areas with good transport links and close to major employment centres. They're common in parts of the country where the cost of living is high, where young professionals moving to town would struggle to get on the property ladder themselves.

There's also a HMO market for tenants on housing benefits, e.g. tenants who have their housing paid for by the local authority, but this type of HMO is less common and requires specialist management. As such, we won't be considering this type of HMO in this chapter, but this could be a good strategy for some people.

Licensing and planning

If you're new to HMOs, you should take some time to read about and understand the different rules and regulations around HMO licensing and how the planning rules works. Here's a quick overview, but you'll need to research this further, if this is a strategy you're planning to execute for yourself.

Planning

Under the current planning system, you'll need to seek full planning permission from your local authority, if you want to convert an existing residential property into a Large HMO, defined in planning law as a shared house occupied by seven or more people. In general, you don't need full planning permission to convert an existing residential property (of use class C3) into a Small HMO (of use class C4), defined as a shared house occupied by three to six people, as planning permission can instead be obtained through your Permitted Development Rights via a prior notification application, which is usually fairly straightforward.

There is one exception to this – full planning permission for a change of use will always be required, even for a Small HMO, in areas where the local council has decided to remove your Permitted Development Rights under what's known as an Article 4 Directive. These Article 4 powers were introduced to give councils the ability to restrict the number of new HMOs coming onto the market in areas with a higher concentration, e.g. areas with lots of student housing. Because local councils can be reluctant to grant planning permission in areas with restrictions in place, you may be better off looking to buy an existing HMO, rather than create one yourself, if you're looking to own a HMO in one of these locations. To check whether Article 4 applies, you can do a quick search online for the area.

Licensing

Under the existing system, a HMO in England and Wales will always need a license if it meets the definition of a large HMO, which is not the same definition used by the planning system. This is known as 'mandatory licensing'. To be a large HMO, the property must have five or more people living there that form more than one household. In addition, local authorities can decide to require that other HMOs (not meeting the large HMO definition) also require a license. This is known as 'additional licensing'. You'll need to check out the website of the local authority where you're planning to set up the HMO to see what licensing rules apply.

Once granted, licenses are generally valid for five years and must be renewed before they run out. Licenses come with certain conditions that need to be met, e.g. gas and electrical safety checks and fire safety measures, and the council can also add other conditions to your license as they deem necessary. If you go to the local authority's website, you can usually find a full list of relevant criteria. If you can't find it online, you can usually request it by calling them up. Before granting you a license, the local council will inspect the property, so you need to make sure you've got a tick against each one of these requirements.

The pros and cons

Running a HMO is much more involved than a regular buy-to-let, but the rewards are also greater. Let's look at some of the pros and cons of this type of investment.

What are the positives?

- Higher ROI and cash flow – If you buy in the right location and you get the marketing and ongoing management right, it will be more profitable than a regular buy-to-let and generate large amounts of cash flow each month. As a rule of thumb, you might expect an ROI of 10% to 15% with HMOs.
- Spreading the tenant risk – With a regular buy-to-let, it's always possible that your tenant will default, leaving you covering all the expenses. With HMOs, this risk is spread across all the tenants living in the property, as you'll likely

be charging on a room-by-room basis. That is, there's much less of a chance all tenants will default at the same time.

- Potential for higher valuations – For larger HMOs, the lender will sometimes value the property based on a profit multiple, rather than on a comparables basis. This can lead to higher valuations and create opportunities to extract some of the cash you've put into the deal, in a BRRR-style strategy akin to that which we covered in play # 30.

What are the negatives?

- It requires a lot more work – There's a lot more work involved in running a HMO, including the marketing, viewings, check-ins, and inventories to keep the property occupied. With so many people living in close proximity, there's also a potential for more tenant issues and more disputes to arise. Even if you decide to use a letting agent, you'll need to stay close to how they're running it, as there are less agents that will do a good job managing HMOs.

- Running costs are higher – The costs of running a HMO are much higher than a traditional buy-to-let. You'll need to pay higher management fees, cover the cost of utilities, subscriptions and council tax, and pay for regular cleaning. The property will be furnished and will get used more extensively, meaning there will likely be greater wear and tear and more maintenance issues.

- There's more regulation – As we've already seen from the discussion above, HMOs are subject to a lot more regulation, be that needing to understand the planning rules around change of use classes or the licensing requirements of the local council where you're planning to operate. You'll need to understand and comply with all these rules and regulations or face big fines.

- Harder to get financing – Lenders like to see some track record of borrowers running a successful property business, before they will finance a HMO, so it can be more difficult to raise financing. In addition, there are fewer lenders that play in this space, and the market is less competitive, so the borrowing costs you'll need to pay will be higher.

A worked example

To understand how the figures work for a HMO, it's useful to look at a worked example. For this case study, I've linked in with a property buddy of mine, as he does a lot of these types of deals. The example below is for a professional HMO he runs in Stevenage, Hertfordshire. He picked this location because it attracts strong rental demand, with Stevenage offering fast rail links into central London. This particular property also had the potential to increase capacity, and purchase prices in the area were still at an attractive level for this type of investment.

Rental income (across five bedrooms)	£2,750

Monthly expenditure

Mortgage interest (5% × £150,000 ÷ 12)	£625
Management fee (14.4% × £2,750)	£396
Repairs and maintenance (10% × £2,750)	£275
Cost of voids (£2,750 × 2 / 52 weeks)	£106
Insurance (£360 p.a. ÷ 12)	£30
Marketing and tenancy set-up (£120 × 5 ÷ 12)	£50
Utilities and subscriptions (5 × £20 pw × 4 weeks)	£400
Cleaning costs (£30 pw × 4 weeks)	£120
Licence for a large HMO (£1,200 ÷ 5 years / 12)	£20
Gas and electrical safety checks	£10
Total expenditure	£2,032

Cash invested

Deposit (25% × £200,000)	£50,000
Stamp duty	£7,500
Refurbishment costs	£25,000
Valuation and survey	£500
Legal expenses	£1,500
Mortgage broker	£500
Total cash invested	£85,000

He approached the research like you would a regular buy-to-let investment. He used Rightmove to estimate the property's market value, and he used websites like spareroom.co.uk to get a feeling for what the monthly rents were for other HMO properties in the area. The key assumptions in the modelling were then as follows: (a) we could secure this three-bedroom, mid-terrace for £200,000, after some negotiation with the seller; (b) we purchase the property with a 75% loan-to-value interest only mortgage at a 5% p.a. interest rate; (c) spending £25,000 will allow us to convert the property into a five-bedroom HMO, with an ensuite for one of the bedrooms and with the other four sharing a bathroom; (d) the total rental income across all five bedrooms will be around £2,750 – £600 per month for the ensuite, £550 per month for the three medium-sized rooms, and £500 per month for the smallest room; (e) we will use a specialist letting agent to manage the HMO, who charges 12% plus VAT of the rent (14.4%) each month plus £120 per room for marketing and setting up new tenancies, which we'll assume is needed once per room per year; (f) repairs and maintenance will cost around 10% of the monthly rent; (g) the cost of utilities and subscriptions, including the water, gas, and electricity and costs like council tax, a TV license, broadband and a Netflix subscription, come to around £20 per room per week; (h) we'll have the property cleaned once per week at a cost of £30 per visit. Converting all these to monthly figures and adding in a few other costs you'll incur with a HMO like this, e.g. insurance premiums, licencing fees and gas and electrical safety testing costs, the numbers then work out as per the figures presented above.

Note that we've also assumed that each room is vacant for an average of two weeks per year, which is pretty close to an assumption of full occupancy for a large HMO like this. In the cash invested section, we've also included some typical allowances for stamp duty, legal expenses, valuation and broker fees. In total, the amount you would need to invest in this particular deal comes to £85,000, not a small sum of money, and it's much more cash intensive than a regular buy-to-let investment. As such, HMOs are not a strategy you can take advantage of without having large chunks of capital to invest. In fact, other than flips, HMO investments are perhaps the most capital intensive of residential property deals.

What results can you achieve?

In this example, we would achieve £2,750 of rental income versus our monthly expenses of £2,032. That is, we would generate £718 of cash flow each month or around £8,616 of annual profit before tax. To see what this equates to as an ROI, we simply take the annual profit of £8,616 ÷ £85,000 (i.e. the money we put into the deal ourselves) which equals 10.1% p.a. before tax. This is a much higher ROI than with a regular buy-to-let investment, and it's possible to push this further, if you're willing to self-manage. For example, taking care of the marketing and day-to-day management yourself would cut your monthly expenses by £446 (that is, the £396 management fee plus £50 for marketing and new tenancy set-ups) and increase your annual profits by £5,352 to £13,968 before tax. As such, if we self-manage, we may be able to achieve an ROI of £13,968 ÷ £85,000, which equals 16.4% p.a. before tax. In this scenario, our monthly cash flow would also increase to £1,164 (£718 plus £446), and it's easy to imagine how you could replace your income quickly by owning a number of these HMO investments. For example, owning three of these HMO properties and investing around £250,000 may allow you to generate a monthly pre-tax income of around £3,500.

How to run a successful HMO

Don't be seduced by the headlines and high ROIs, running a profitable HMO is a challenge for most people, and it needs to be done with thought and care. To get this right, you'll need to have the right mindset, run this as a professional business venture, and give it the time and attention it needs to thrive. Here are some of my top tips for running a successful HMO investment.

- Pick the right location – If you pick the right location for the HMO, everything else will be a lot easier. For student HMOs, you'll need to pick an area close to a university; for professional HMOs, you'll want an area that's close to good transport links and major employment centres. Use the existing stock of HMO properties as your guide, and stray outside these boundaries at your peril.

- Get the refurb right – Gone are the days of low-quality HMOs and student lets. Today's HMO tenants expect quality accommodation and nice furnishings, as well as add-ons like broadband, free Wi-Fi and Netflix, as standard. To make your life easier, you'll want to configure the property in a way that maximises the available living space and fits in the largest number of bedrooms. Good design is essential to getting the refurbish right and turning a profit.

- Use a specialist letting agent – If you're new to HMOs, it can be a good idea to use a specialist letting agent to manage the property for you, even if you plan to manage the property yourself later on. That way, you can see how it's done and learn from them. Choose an agent that specialises in HMOs, as you're unlikely to get a good service from your regular high street letting agent.

- Streamline your management – If you're going to self-manage, there's lots you can do to streamline the day-to-day management. For example, you can batch viewings into a single day to cut down the amount of visits needed, you can set up a website with a house manual that gives details of how to operate the appliances, alarm system, heating controls, etc, and you can go paperless with all documents and contracts. Technology can also help in other ways – for example, you can send automated text reminders about paying the rent, install a heating system controlled by an app to keep heating costs down, and use keyless entry systems or a master key system to help with access.

- Get the right tenant mix – Getting the right tenant mix will help to reduce the number of tenant issues. Grouping similar tenant types together will help, as will carefully vetting their references to make sure they don't have a history. Treat your tenants as your customers and strive to make their experience a good one - satisfied tenants will stay longer and take better care of the things.

- Have the right mindset – If you're getting into HMOs hoping that you can pull off big returns without putting in any extra work, then you'll be disappointed. However, if you approach it with the right mindset, knowing it will be hard, but aiming to refine your systems and processes over time to optimise the business, then the whole experience will be much more satisfying.

Common pitfalls and mistakes

The common pitfalls and mistakes that can arise with HMOs are when investors treat it like an extension of regular buy-to-let and don't take the time to acquire the technical knowledge needed to be successful or to research and understand the market they're planning to enter. Here are some of the other common pitfalls and mistakes investors make with this particular strategy.

- Breaching the terms of the lease – If you're buying a leasehold property, then you need to check the terms of the lease before you buy. Many leases prohibit subletting in the manner required, which means you wouldn't be able to use it as a HMO. It's for this reason that most HMOs are freehold houses.
- Not getting a specialist mortgage – You need to take out the right mortgage product, which means you'll need a mortgage specifically for HMOs. Interest rates on HMO mortgages are higher, and the choice is also more restricted. This is an area where working with a good broker can really help you get the right product and secure the best financing on offer.
- Falling down on compliance – As we've seen earlier in this chapter, running a successful HMO requires full compliance with all rules and regulations, including planning laws and licensing requirements. There can be big fines for those who fail to comply, so it's not a strategy you should attempt without the right education and background.

As a final word, HMOs and multi-lets offer the potential for outsized returns in a way that no other residential property investment can, but earning those returns is only possible through hard work and hard-won knowledge. The core principle at work with the HMO strategy is the same time versus money trade-off at play in so many other aspects of life, so if you're time poor or not up for the extra work involved, then it's probably not a strategy for you.

Play # 43 – How to use lease options

Lisa and Andy were at the start of their investment journey, and they didn't have lots of savings. They were keen to do something, anything, to get started in property – they'd seen the success others had in the last boom – but their ambition far exceeded their capital. That's when Andy stumbled across an article on lease options, which claimed investors using this approach could get started right away with little money down. It sounded perfect, but was it too good to be true? There must be some catch. When something sounds too good to be true, it usually is. They'd have to find out more.

Exploring your options

Our next play, how to use lease options, is about one of the more complex ideas in property investment. Like joint ventures, lease options are a popular training topic for property gurus who like to charge lots of money for expensive courses, and this is because they offer a way of getting started in property using little to no money down – a great benefit if you're trying to sell courses. However, lease options are actually quite a niche strategy, and although they can work well in certain circumstances, they can be difficult to execute, and finding opportunities can be more like a second job. In this play, we're going to look at what lease options are, how you can use them to invest in property, and at some of the common pitfalls and mistakes with this strategy.

An introduction to lease options

What is a lease option?

Unless you work in finance, lease options are one of the more esoteric and hard-to-understand strategies in property. In this introduction, we're going to take it slow, start with some definitions, and build your knowledge from there.

A lease option is a legal agreement that allows you to 'control' a property and generate rental profits by letting the property out. It also gives you the right (but not the obligation) to buy the property for an agreed upon price within a specified timeframe. There are two bits that make up a lease option:

- The lease – You agree to pay the owner a monthly payment in exchange for the right to let out the property to a tenant and make a profit.
- The option – You agree the price at which you can buy the property from the owner at a later date and the time when this option will expire.

If you do work in finance, then it probably suffices to say that a lease option is a lease agreement overlaid with a long call option, with the strike price equal to the agreed purchase price for the property.

When you're fleshing out the details of a lease option, there are four headline terms that need to be agreed upon by both parties. Let's take a look at these items in a bit more detail along with some rationale for how they're determined.

1. The monthly payment – The monthly payment should be the sum the owner needs each month to cover their mortgage and other costs, e.g. ground rent, service charge, buildings insurance, etc.
2. The purchase price – This is the price you can buy the property in the future, if you decide to exercise the option. It's usually set at or above the market value of the property – we'll come onto why later in the chapter.
3. The length of the agreement – Usually the length of the lease agreement and option expiry date are set equal to each other. At the end of the agreement, if

you haven't exercised your option to buy the property, then you'll hand the property back to the owner.

4. The option premium – It's typical to make an upfront payment to the owner at the time the agreement is put in place. A non-zero option premium makes the option legally binding (consideration is then in both directions) and helps the owner cover their expenses, e.g. legal fees and the cost of moving out.

If you're new to lease options, you might be thinking that all this already sounds a little complicated, but it's actually even more complex than simply agreeing the headline terms above. For example, you need to specify in detail which party will cover what types of costs and, if the length of the agreement is long, whether the monthly payment will increase in some way to take into account the longer-term impact of inflation on the owner's costs. All of this needs careful consideration.

Why lease options work

With the basics out of the way, let's look at why lease options work and what they achieve for the various parties involved in the agreement. To help, let's look at a simple worked example from the perspective of the buyer and the seller.

The buyer's perspective

Suppose you agree a lease option with the owner of a two-bedroom house that has the following deal terms: (a) the market value of the property is £100,000; (b) you have the option to buy the property for £110,000 – that is, the strike price is £110,000; (c) you agree to pay the owner £350 per month to lease the property, which covers their mortgage payments; (d) the option and the lease agreement both have a length of five years, which you chose to be the end of the fixed-rate period on the owner's existing mortgage; (e) you pay the owner £1,500 to help cover their legal and moving costs. You also agree to cover the cost of repairs and buildings insurance. Adding in a few other typical costs that might be expected for a rental property like this, the numbers then work out as follows.

Rental income	£725

Monthly expenditure

Lease payment to the owner	£350
Management fee (11% × £725)	£80
Repairs and maintenance (5% × £725)	£36
Cost of voids (£725 × 2 / 52 weeks)	£28
Buildings insurance (£240 p.a. ÷ 12)	£20
Public liability insurance (£60 p.a. ÷ 12)	£5
Marketing and tenancy set-up (£360 p.a. ÷ 12)	£30
Total expenditure	£549

I've assumed the property would rent out for £725 per month, is vacant for two weeks per year, which is akin to a tenant staying for two years on average and then the house taking a month or so to let out again, and I've included some other typical costs, assuming you use an agent to market the property. In this example, you would achieve £725 of rental income versus your monthly expenses of £549. That is, you would generate £176 of cash flow each month or around £2,112 of annual profit before tax.

Now let's look forward to the potential situations you might face in five years. There are two possible scenarios. (1) The property is worth less than £110,000, let's say £105,000 for illustration purposes. You probably wouldn't want to buy it for £110,000, more than its market value, so you let your option expire and you return the property to the owner. In this case, you'll have made £10,560 (£2,112 profit per annum × 5 years) less the £1,500 upfront payment for an overall profit of £9,060. (2) The property value has increased, say to £120,000. Here, it's likely you would want to buy the property for £110,000, that is, at a £10,000 discount to its market value, either to run as a buy-to-let or to sell on for an immediate profit. You'll also still have made £9,060 in rental profits over the period. It's also worth noting that lease options are typically structured so that you can buy the property at any time in the option period, not just at the option end date.

To quickly summarise, provided you structure the deal correctly and you get the details right, lease options can be great from the buyer's perspective. The deal itself requires little money down, just the upfront option premium and your own legal fees, and you get to let out the property each month and make rental profits as if you owned the property already. If the market value of the property goes up in value over the option period, you gain once the price goes north of the agreed purchase price, giving you access to the upside. At the same time, if prices don't increase, you're under no legal obligation to buy the property, and you can simply hand the property back at the end of the agreement term.

That brings us to the next question. If lease options are great for buyers, why would the owner ever agree to such a one-sided deal where they are giving away all the market upside. Let's look at that a bit closer.

The seller's perspective

In general, sellers prefer not to enter into these types of lease option agreements, for the reasons highlighted. They're committing themselves to a fixed sale price and giving away their upside if the market does well; they're also handing over their property to a complete stranger who's under no legal obligation to follow through with the purchase. Yes, they're getting an upfront payment, but this is generally small relative to the other sums being discussed.

For all these reasons and more, owner's will generally only agree to take part in this type of deal if they have no other viable options. The most typical scenario is where the owner is in 'negative equity' – meaning that the outstanding balance on their mortgage is greater than the property is currently worth – and they have some sort of pressing reason why they need to move out quickly, be that a change in circumstances or financial difficulties. Using the example above, suppose that the owner bought the property for £120,000 and took out a 90% loan-to-value mortgage, meaning they still owe around £108,000. Since they bought the house, property prices in the area have fallen, meaning the house is now worth only £100,000, and the owner suddenly needs to relocate for work reasons. In this situation, the owner is unable push for a sale quickly by lowering the price, as it wouldn't raise enough to clear the outstanding mortgage balance of £108,000. They also couldn't sell at the current market value of £100,000 unless they had £8,000 in cash and were willing to pay the bank the difference. They could move out and rent the property to a tenant, but this is quite a lot of work and still leaves them on the hook for the mortgage payments, so they could still get into a bit of trouble, if their tenant defaults – not a risk many people are willing to take when their finances are running a bit thin.

To summarise, most owners willing to consider lease options are backed into a corner in some way by their personal circumstances. Most would like to sell the property and get rid of the issue completely, but they're not able to do so. Some owners in this situation will go down the lettings route, despite the hassle and perceived riskiness. However, those that don't may be grateful to a third party that's willing to get involved and help them find their way out of a messy, complex situation that could leave them in dire straits. In short, for the seller, the appeal of a lease option is that it can help them extricate themselves from a difficult situation.

How to find opportunities

Let's face it, you're unlikely to find lease option deals by browsing on Rightmove or talking to agents, so finding opportunities to use these techniques is by far the biggest obstacle to success. As you can see from the above, to find an owner who'd be interested in this, you're looking for someone who is in negative equity and who needs to move quickly. So, you need to target your search on areas where there are likely to be owner occupiers in negative equity. Back in 2010, right after the last property crash, this would have been much of the UK. At the time of writing, with prices bouncing back steadily since 2010, few areas would meet this general condition, and you're likely to be restricted mainly to parts of the North East and North West of England as areas where buyers could still be underwater. In addition, could also target any local markets which have recently seen a tumble in prices due to specific local factors.

Once you've chosen your target areas, that's when the real graft begins. You'll need to identify people in those areas who need to move house quickly and would be open to a discussion about lease options. That's not an easy task, and the most common approaches including the following:

- Direct mail and leafleting – You can write letters to everyone in a particular area, be that a town, a number of streets or a cherry-picked apartment block, where you know there are property owners in negative equity. You need to provide your contact details and hope someone reaches out to you.
- Running online adverts – Nowadays, it's straightforward to set targeted ad campaigns on Google or Facebook. Depending on the platform, you'll either be able to have your adverts shown to a demographic group of your choosing or in response to your chosen keywords.
- Develop a local network – Finally, you could try to build a network of contacts in the area that you're targeting. This could be a network of estate and letting agents that might help you identify opportunities in exchange for placing the ongoing property management business with them. Alternatively, if you live locally, it could be a network of other investors or a social group.

None of this is easy, and it's likely to take significant upfront and persistent effort to yield any positive leads at all. Then, once you have some leads, you'll still have the challenge of turning those leads into actual deals, which won't be easy as the solution is complex, requires a good deal of explanation, and the seller will likely be going through some changes or personal difficulties.

The biggest single factor in converting leads into sales will be your ability to establish trust. Without it, there's no hope of getting a deal like this over the line. You'll need to do everything you can to establish and maintain a good reputation. You should be open and transparent in all your dealings and explain clearly what the owner is giving up and all the things that can go wrong. Think 'no surprises'. Where you have them, provide references and testimonials.

Documenting the agreement

As we've already seen, a lease option consists of two separate legal agreements: firstly, there's the option agreement, which details the option length, the agreed purchase price or strike price, and any upfront payment or premium that's due; secondly, there's the lease (or management) agreement, which states how much you'll pay to the owner each month, who's responsible for what costs, and any conditions you need to abide by in the letting and ongoing management of the property. You may also want to put in place some sort of restriction on title, to prevent the owner selling the property to someone else.

All of this means you should work with an experienced solicitor to make sure the agreements you put in place are robust and legally binding. You'll want to make sure the owner takes legal advice of their own from a separate solicitor, so that they can't cry foul later on, if they decide to back out of the deal. When you're negotiating the key terms, try to argue for as long an option period as you can, to allow time for capital growth, and try to make sure the upfront payment amount has some rationale, i.e. a sum to cover their legal fees and moving costs. When it comes to agreeing the purchase price or strike price, you want this to be as low as possible, so that your option is 'in-the-money' sooner, but in general a sensible figure is often the outstanding balance on the owner's mortgage. Likewise, when it comes to agreeing the monthly payment, you want this to be as low as possible, but the minimum you'll likely get away with is whatever sum the owner needs to cover their costs and leave them in a neutral position.

Finally, it's worth emphasising that the legal agreements you put in place need to be crystal clear about what costs will be borne by the seller and by the buyer. Ideally, you would structure it simply, say with the owner being responsible only for their mortgage costs and the buyer picking up all other costs. If you go down this route, you may want some appropriate representations or warranties in the agreement to ensure the owner fulfils their obligations, like making the mortgage payments, and to force them to disclosure any relevant background before the transaction, e.g. any unpaid utility bills, service charges, or ground rents.

Common pitfalls and mistakes

Given their complexity, there are lots of potential pitfalls and mistakes investors can make with lease options. Here are a few common ones:

- Ignoring the terms of the lease – If the property is a leasehold property, then you need to check the terms of the lease before you buy. Many leases have restrictions around subletting the property, e.g. that the property can only be sublet in full, and you need to make sure you comply with these.

- Not seeking the lender's agreement – You need to make sure the owner has permission from their lender to let the property out in this manner. In most cases, the owner will be on a residential mortgage, so they'll need the lender's 'consent to let' before entering a lease option agreement. Because they're in negative equity, the owner is unlikely to be able to re-mortgage.

- Operating on thin margins – The operating cash flows for these deals can be thin. The owner will likely be on a repayment mortgage, and their mortgage payments will be higher than if you bought the property on an interest only mortgage. However, you'll need to pay them enough to clear their expenses. In practice, these deals often only work in higher yielding locations.

- Failing to document the agreement – We've talked at length above about the importance of getting a legal agreement in place. However, it's also important that you work with a solicitor that's experienced with lease options. You can't work with just any conveyancing solicitor; you need to work with a specialist who knows the ins and outs and who can help you structure a deal to protect the interests of all parties. The best way to find one is by networking with other property investors or via a recommendation.

- Relying on the legal agreements – Just because you have the legal paperwork in place doesn't mean that the deal is done. In practice, you're relying on the owner's cooperation as long as the agreements are running. This exposes you to risks like the owner not paying the mortgage and the lender repossessing the property, the owner refusing to go through with the transaction after you exercise the option, and the owner failing to cover any ongoing expenses allocated to them in the agreements. Legal action to enforce the contracts is likely to be expensive and may not be worth it, in practice. So, you should try to maintain a good working relationship with the owner at all times and keep them informed of developments regularly.

- Playing fast and loose with the ethics – There's no getting around it, this is a strategy that's built on identifying sellers in a degree of financial difficulty, and with that comes a duty to ensure you're operating ethically. You should be open and transparent in all your dealings with the owners. If you're not, this will likely come back to bite you.

As an aside to the third bullet, there are ways to structure the deal to simulate the impact of the seller switching to a buy-to-let mortgage, e.g. you could agree to a refund from the seller to the buyer equal to the outstanding mortgage balance at the date the owner enters into the lease option and the outstanding balance at the date the option is executed. This refund would effectively compensate you for the fact that you've been paying the seller's full mortgage payment each month and they've been accruing equity in the property as a result. The downside of this structure is that you only get the refund if you actually buy the property, which doesn't help with the thin operating cash flows over the hold period, though it does give you a bit more upside if you do buy the property.

Redux

One extension of this strategy that's useful to know about is renting the property to a 'tenant buyer'. A tenant buyer is someone who would like to buy the property, but who doesn't have a deposit just yet. In this situation, you can make a separate agreement with this tenant buyer that you will sell them your option to buy the property for a predetermined price at a time of their choosing, up to the option expiry date. In our earlier example say, you might agree that the tenant buyer can buy your option off you for £10,000 whenever they choose. In practice, once the market value of the property rises higher than £120,000, they may be interested in buying that option. For example, say the tenant buyer believes the market value to be £125,000, they can buy the option for £10,000 and execute it to buy the property from the owner for the agreed purchase price of £110,000. In total, they'll have paid £120,000 for a property they believe is worth £125,000, and so they've gotten a great deal.

But what do you as an investor get out of this agreement? Firstly, you get a longer-term tenant who will treat the property as if it were their own, meaning lower repair costs and less voids. Secondly, you get to sell the property and make a capital gain without ever having to put down any of your own money. Last but not least, you avoid a boatload of transaction-related costs, including stamp duty, legal fees and financing costs, by not having to buy the property before selling it on to someone else. This is ideal if your main motivation for entering into a lease option agreement was to profit from a short-term uptick in the wider market and you had no real intention of owning the property yourself as a buy-to-let.

Wrapping it up

Lease options are much talked about in property circles, but rarely used in reality. This has as much to do with the complexity of the strategy as it does the difficulty of scouting out opportunities in a cost-effective manner. The technical nature of the discussions you'll need to have with owners makes this a strategy not well-suited for beginners, and there's a lot that can go wrong, if you're not able to put the deal on a solid legal footing and if you fail to manage the relationship with the owner well over time. That said, the theory behind lease options is well worth knowing, as you may stumble across an opportunity in another area where these ideas would work well and could add value. In addition, there will be points in the property cycle, usually just after a crash, where this strategy is much easier to implement. As such, it's worth having lease options as one of the tools in your toolkit when the market crashes. Just because you know how to do the macarena, doesn't mean you'll have the chance to bust it out at every party.

Play # 44 – The rent-to-rent cash flow play

We've all heard of accidental landlords, but Claire was an accidental rent-to-renter. When she finished her degree in Sheffield, she didn't know what to do with herself. She'd was living in a student HMO on the outskirts of town and about to move back in with her parents, when a chance discussion with her landlord threw her an opportunity. He was tired of managing the HMO, and he wondered if she would take over. If she took take of the repairs and paid him a fixed rent, she could take the upside from letting the rooms to her fellow students. That's the moment Claire's rent-to-rent business was born.

The hottest topic in property

Our next play is about one of the hottest topics in property, rent-to-rent (or R2R). It's a topic shrouded in mystery and which has sired plenty of training courses, often run by property guru types with questionable credentials. Take a browse through any of the online property forums, and there's bound to be a section on rent-to-rent and pages of debate about it. Is it really a great way to make money, and how much work does it involve? How do you put the agreements on a strong legal footing, and is it legal in the first place? Is it just another property fad which makes more money for training course providers than for practitioners? Over the next few pages, you'll get answers to all these questions and more. I'll provide an overview of the rent-to-rent strategy, look at the pros and cons of this approach, and describe two commonly used rent-to-rent models. We'll run through some of the keys to success and common pitfalls and mistakes. After that, you'll have all the background you need to decide whether it's a strategy for you and whether it lives up to all the hype.

An introduction to rent-to-rent

What is rent-to-rent?

Despite all of the headlines and hullabaloo, rent-to-rent is actually quite a niche property strategy not practiced by many people at all. It's also not really property investment, as at no point do you actually buy and own the property yourself. The general concept is fairly straightforward and involves two parts:

- you rent a property from a landlord long-term
- you then rent the property out to tenants yourself

To make a profit, the rent you charge to your tenants needs to be higher than the rent you pay to the landlord. To make the numbers work, you'll need to rent the property from the landlord for between 75% and 100% of its single-let market rent, then let the property out in a way that generates higher revenues than a single let. We'll come back to this point shortly.

The different parties

As the rent-to-rent manager, you're effectively taking control of the property, and you're running it as if you were a landlord who's opted to self-manage. That is, you're going to be in charge of marketing the property, letting it out to tenants, and taking care of all aspects of the ongoing management, including maintenance and repairs. For the rent-to-rent manager, it can be a great deal, as you get to let the property out as if it were your own and generate a cash income.

In order for rent-to-rent to be a win-win, the landlord needs to get something from the deal too. Usually what the landlord gets out of this is a 'guaranteed rent' payable for an extended period of time, say three to five years. Yes, the landlord's income will be lower than if they let the property themselves, but the deal gives them certainty. They no longer need to worry about voids, repair bills, and unpaid rent – as the rent-to-rent manager, you're taking on these risks. The landlord only has to worry about whether you'll continue to meet your obligations. The other advantage for the landlord is that they don't have to put in any effort.

The pros and cons

Rent-to-rent has a lot in common with some of the more time intensive property strategies like running a HMO or self-managing a holiday let, as the skills needed are similar. In fact, people who tend to have great success with rent-to-rent have often been successful with these other strategies first, and they already have the systems and processes in place to run the business smoothly from the word go. Let's look at some of the pros and cons of rent-to-rent as a strategy.

What are the positives?

- You don't need a lot of money – As we've already seen, property investment generally requires lots of capital to invest. However, with rent-to-rent, you're not actually buying the property, so there's no need to save for a deposit. In fact, you typically only need enough cash to cover the first few months' rent and to fund the cost of any works needed before you let the property out.

- There's no need for a mortgage – Building on the above, because you're not buying the property, there's no need for a mortgage. That means rent-to-rent can appeal to investors who may struggle to get a mortgage, perhaps due to personal circumstances, limited earnings, or poor credit history.

- No purchase costs – Once again, you're not buying the property, which cuts out many of the costs you'd normally incur with buy-to-let and other such property deals. There's no stamp duty, lender valuation fees, survey costs, legal expenses and mortgage broker fees. You'll want to have a solicitor look over the rental or management agreement, but this should be inexpensive.

- Deals are quick to execute – Because there's no need to go through a lengthy conveyancing process, rent-to-rent deals can be quick to execute, provided all parties are on board. It's possible to tie a deal up in a matter of weeks, rather than months.

What are the negatives?

- No capital growth upside – With rent-to-rent, you never own the property, so you won't benefit from any increase in the property's value over time. For many people, capital growth is the principal reason they invest in property, and this is what makes rent-to-rent unattractive for many investors.

- It takes a lot of work – There's a lot more work involved than a regular buy-to-let investment, including all the marketing and day-to-day management. Without a doubt, the work involved is akin to creating a second job – you're giving yourself the job of being a letting agent. Even if the pay is good, it's still a job, so it's not a strategy for those who are time-poor.

- The margins can be thin – The cash flows for rent-to-rent deals can be thin. The landlord will likely want to be paid somewhere close to the market rent, and even if they do offer you a discount, you'll need to get your modelling right and work hard to make sure there's enough cash left to cover all your expenses and leave you with a profit.

- Risk without the control – As the rent-to-rent manager, you're taking on all the risks of property – voids, maintenance and repairs, tenants defaulting – and you need to pay the landlord no matter what. At the same time, however, you're not in full control of the property, e.g. the landlord could stop paying their mortgage and the lender may repossess the property.

- It can be difficult to sell the concept – Rent-to-rent is still a niche property strategy, and it can be difficult for landlords to understand. In addition, some landlords just don't like the idea of giving up control, and some just won't like the idea of their property being used in this way. For all these reasons, it can be difficult to get landlords to buy in to the concept.

Getting started with rent-to-rent

Two rent-to-rent models

In order to strike profitable deals, you'll need to find a way to rent the property for more than you're paying to the landlord. In general, this isn't possible using a single let model, as the margins are usually too thin, so you'll need to use another model. There are two basic rent-to-rent models.

1. Turn the property into a HMO

The most common model, the original recipe if you will, is to take a family home with three or four bedrooms and turn it into a HMO. You'll be able to increase the top line rental income just by renting out the rooms separately; if you spend some money converting the property, say by turning a reception room into an extra bedroom, then you may be able push your top line even further.

With this model, you would typically look to pay the landlord the full single-let market rent, or an amount close to that, and then spend some time and money upfront converting the property and configuring it so that it works as a HMO. One point to clarify here is that you absolutely do need to be straight and open with the landlord about what you're doing and how you plan to use the property. This is a non-negotiable, and you'll likely get yourself into all kinds of hot water, if you try to perpetrate any ruse or deception.

We've covered HMOs at length in play # 42. But, as a reminder, when you're running the HMO, you'll likely be responsible for all the bills and extra costs that come with running a HMO, which will increase your running costs – you need to factor these extra costs into your calculations. You'll also need to comply with all planning and licensing requirements, when setting up the HMO.

It's also possible, and we'll come back to this, to strike rent-to-rent deals with existing HMO landlords. For example, say you meet a landlord with several HMOs who's been in the game for years and is growing tired of the work and the hassle involved but isn't quite ready to sell up. You could make an offer to run their HMO for them, and you could structure the arrangement as a rent-to-rent deal.

2. Turn the property into serviced accommodation

Another common rent-to-rent model that's gaining some traction in the market is to turn the property into serviced accommodation. As we saw in play # 29, the term serviced accommodation is an umbrella term for furnished accommodation that's available for both short and long term let, but which tends to focus on the corporate rental market. So, your tenants might be contractors moving for work, employees on secondment, or corporate executives on a relocation programme. The average nightly rate you receive will be higher than a single let, which makes it possible to increase the top line rental income.

With this second model, you would typically look to pay the landlord less than the full market rent for a single let, say around the 75% to 90% level. In general, short-stay guests tend to take better care of the property, and the property will likely be getting a weekly clean, so it's going to be kept in good condition all year-round. That means it's an easier sell to the landlord, and with a little bit of effort you should be able to secure a small discount to the single-let market rent.

We've covered serviced accommodation in play # 29. But just as a reminder, when you're running the property as serviced accommodation, there will be some set up costs, as you'll need to furnish the property to a high standard, and there will be a lot of work to do around the day-to-day marketing and management of the property, including dealing with any changeovers. As with HMOs, you'll also need to cover the cost of utilities and pay for cleaning and fresh linen each week, so the running costs are higher. All of this needs to be factored into your calculations.

How to find opportunities

When rent-to-rent is done well, it creates a win for all parties: the landlord gets a guaranteed rental income, with virtually no hassle; the rent-to-rent manager gets to run a business they like and generate a cash flow with little-to-no money down. However, it's still a niche strategy, and most landlords are comfortable managing the property themselves or using a letting agent. So how do you find rent-to-rent opportunities and landlords that would be interested in working with you. There are lots of ways to go about this, but here are three of the most common ones:

- Pitch your offer to letting agents – The easiest way to a large pool of landlords is via letting agents. If you're going to pitch your offer to a letting agent, you'll need to explain what you're offering and what's in it for the landlord and the agent. Many agents won't understand it and most won't like it – you're doing their job for them. To get around this, rent-to-rent deals set up via agents tend to be structured so that the agent continues to take their management fee, despite doing none of the work, which can be somewhat inefficient.

- Approach landlords directly – There are lots of ways to approach landlords directly to see if they are interest in what you're offering. If you're looking for properties in city centres that could be run as serviced accommodation, then you can browse the portals like Rightmove and Zoopla, as well as holiday let websites like airbnb, to find potential leads and contacts directly. Likewise, if you're looking for existing HMOs that are tired and run-down with a view to pitching your services to the owner, try looking for leads on websites like spareroom.co.uk and gumtree.co.uk, where rooms might be advertised.

- Set yourself up as a managing agent – Finally, it's worth discussing the option of setting yourself up as a managing agent. Yes, it's potentially a lot of hard work, and you'll need to have a strategy in place for how you build your presence and how you advertise your services to landlords, but if you get this strategy right, landlords will come to you. You're effectively setting yourself up as a specialist letting agency dealing solely with serviced accommodation or HMOs, with a fee model that's based solely around a guaranteed rent.

All of these options require a good deal of effort, and making any of them work in practice will require an aptitude for relationship-building and strong sales skills. You'll also need to have strong systems in place for keeping track of any leads and the tenacity and grit to see these deals through to completion.

How to be successful with rent-to-rent

Now that we have a better feel for the different rent-to-rent models and how to find opportunities, let's look at how to be successful with rent-to-rent.

- Stick to your local area – With rent-to-rent deals, the operating margins and cash flows are too thin to involve a letting agent, so you'll be managing the day-to-day running of the properties yourself. In order to make the best use of your time, you should stick to a well-defined local area. It's not uncommon for rent-to-rent managers to look after several properties on the same street.

- Pick a tenant type – As we saw with HMOs in play # 42, it's important to pick a target tenant type. You could create HMOs for young professionals, serviced accommodation for contractors, or something else entirely – it's really up to you. However, you should think carefully about what type of accommodation will work best in the local area that you operate in. If you can, it's best to stick to a single tenant type and refine your marketing, systems and processes to serve this market.

- Get your numbers right – As with any property strategy, getting it right is all about the numbers. You need to do your research to understand the local demand and typical market rents; you'll also need to build a realistic model of the likely running costs. Do this before you negotiate with the landlord on the rent, otherwise you won't know what room you have for manoeuvre.

- Use the right legal agreements – The legal nature of the agreements behind rent-to-rent deals can be complex. Sometimes you'll want a lease agreement in place; other times you'll want to use a management contract. You need to use the right one for the situation and make sure you have all the important terms documented and in writing. This is to protect you and the landlord. Having good legal agreements in place will make sure the landlord can't just take the property back at a moment's notice, leaving you hanging. It will also give transparency about the obligations of all parties and which parties are responsible for meeting what costs.

- Build up your systems and processes – The day-to-day management required with rent-to-rent strategies can be intensive. You'll need good systems and processes in place for marketing and finding new tenants, a good back-office to manage check-ins, new tenancy set-up, and check-outs, and a great team around you to manage the day-to-day running of the business and make sure you stay compliant with all those legal requirements.

- Use technology to make your life easier – Whether it's a master key system you put in place to avoid walking around with a big bunch of keys like a jailor, a cloud storage system where you store all your contracts and documents, or an online booking system to arrange cleaning at your properties, you should use technology to help you operate your rent-to-rent business efficiently.

Common pitfalls and mistakes

The main pitfalls and mistakes with rent-to-rent typically arise when people treat the whole venture a bit too casually. Here are some common ones:

- Running before you can walk – If you've never managed a property before, it might be difficult for you to suddenly take on the management of a HMO. There's a natural tension with rent-to-rent in that it's most appealing for investors at the start of their property journey with little available capital, but it's better suited to established investors with the systems and processes in place to make it a success. If you're new to property and considering this strategy, start small, perhaps with a small HMO, and build up from there.

- Breaching the terms of the lease – If you're using a leasehold property, then you need to check the terms of the lease before you proceed with any legal agreements. Many leases prohibit subletting on a short-term basis, e.g. less than three months, which means you wouldn't be able to use it as serviced accommodation. In addition, many leases wouldn't allow use as a HMO.

- Breaching the terms of the mortgage – You need to make sure the deal you're putting in place with the landlord doesn't breach the terms of their mortgage.

Most buy-to-let mortgages wouldn't allow you to run the property as a HMO, and many wouldn't allow you to use the property as a short-term let either.

- Ignoring planning permissions – If you're planning on converting a property into a large HMO, then you may need to seek planning permission. If you're thinking of going down this route, make sure you contact the local council in your area and research the requirements thoroughly before you proceed. We covered the rules around HMO planning in detail in play # 42.

- Falling down on compliance – You need to make sure you're complying with all the rules and regulations around HMOs. If you're new to HMOs, make sure you research these thoroughly and go back to play # 42 for an overview. You need to understand and comply with any licensing requirements. You'll also need to get the right insurance policies in place, to make sure your business is properly covered.

Reversal

Although it's talked about a lot in property circles, rent-to-rent is an advanced property strategy. It's legally technical and can be risky, if you don't know what you're doing, so you should make sure you take good legal advice, if you're going to operate in this area. It's not a strategy you should undertake lightly, and you need to know what you're getting into with this type of venture.

Rent-to-rent is also not a strategy for investors looking to make easy money. Although it doesn't require lots of money to get started, it's a hands-on business model and not something you should get involved with unless you're up for the extra work involved and you think you'll enjoy it. If you're more of a "set it and forget it" type of property investor with little time on their hands, this strategy might not be for you.

Play # 45 – Investing in commercial property

When falling yields made buy-to-let property in his local area unattractive, long-time landlord Philip realised he needed a new approach. In the past, he'd thought about commercial property, but he'd never taken the plunge. He wondered if now was the time to give it another try. He knew commercial property was vulnerable to the ups and downs of the economy, but he also knew it could offer great yields and a stable income stream, if he got it right. He'd need to start small and learn his craft, just as he had with residential in the early days. He'd also need to get the right team in place him around.

A whole other ballgame

Many property investors go their whole careers investing solely in residential property, and there's nothing wrong with that whatsoever – there's always going to be demand for places to live. But for the more adventurous property investors, there's a whole other ball game with a slightly different set of rules that can offer even greater returns, if you learn how to play it well. That's what out next play, investing in commercial property, is all about. There's so much to talk about here, commercial property investment is worth a book or two in its own right, so we're not going to be able to do it justice in a few short pages. However, what I do hope is that this play will spark your interest and teach you enough about the basics to enable you to go out and learn more. In this play, I'm going to give you a short introduction to commercial property. We're going to look at the different types of commercial property, at the pros and cons of this type of investment, and at some of the keys to success, if you're thinking of branching out and making the transition from residential to commercial property. Getting your knowledge and skills up to scratch in a whole new sport is never going to be easy, but it's all to play for, and today is as good a day as any to make a start.

An introduction to commercial property

What is commercial property?

Commercial property includes any property occupied for the purposes of running a business. At the smaller end of the market, it includes pubs, convenience stores, dental practices, and the like; at the larger end of the market, it includes things like large office blocks, logistic parks and distribution centres, and purpose-built shopping centres. It's also possible to buy mixed-use developments, for example, shops with flats above, which are a mix of commercial and residential. In general, it's common to divide commercial property up into the following categories:

- Offices – This includes office buildings rented out to a variety of businesses, e.g. professional services firms, as well as serviced offices.
- Retail – This includes everything from mom-and-pop convenience stores and regular high street shops to big supermarket chains and shopping malls.
- Industrial – Includes logistic parks, distribution centres and storage facilities, industrial parks, manufacturing and processing plants, etc.
- Leisure – This category includes businesses like hotels and hostels, pubs and bars, restaurants, cafes, and take-aways and sports facilities.
- Healthcare – Includes medical centres, private hospitals and other medical facilities like doctors' surgeries, dental practices and nursing homes.

Each of these categories can be seen as an investment class in its own right, with their own unique characteristics and risk-return profile. It's not uncommon, even within commercial property, to find investors who stick to one or two of these classes, owing to the specialist knowledge they've built up in a particular sector or geographical area and how the risk-return profile of that category suits their mindset, investment objectives and personality traits.

In the UK, much of the available stock of commercial property is actually owned by institutional investors, like insurance companies and pension funds, and by commercial property funds. This is partly due to the fact that commercial property can be more difficult to get into for individual investors. However, it's also got a lot to do with the larger deal sizes and larger amount of capital needed, as well as the specialist knowledge required to be successful. That being said, there's no fundamental reason individual investors can't get involved this space, and many do.

The pros and cons

As we've already acknowledged, investing in commercial property is a different proposition than residential property investment. It has more to do with finding a local need and satisfying that demand – that is, thinking like an entrepreneur – than it does running a property rental business. That being said, there is some crossover in the skills needed, particularly in things like finding and building the investment case, putting a value on what the property is worth, and financing the deal. Let's look at the pros and cons of this kind of investment.

What are the positives?

- Higher yields and cash flows – Commercial property provides higher yields and stronger cash flows than residential property. So, commercial property can be attractive as a long-term investment, for those looking for income.
- Longer lease lengths – Standing at around seven years, the average length of a commercial property lease is much longer than the six to twelve-month AST you'll get with residential buy-to-let investments. Commercial property can, therefore, provide investors with a stable income stream over the long term. Of course, finding the right tenant then becomes even more important.

- Full repairing and insuring – Many commercial leases are what's known as 'fully repairing and insuring', which means the tenant is responsible for 100 per cent of the costs, including any repair costs. This is a big difference versus residential, where the landlord is responsible for repairs. In addition, at the end of the lease, the tenant is also responsible for putting right any damage or defects under what's known as a 'dilapidations' provision.

- Inflation-linked income stream – Commercial leases will usually contain rent review provisions requiring the rent charged to be revisited periodically, say every three to five years. Rents are often linked to either wider market rents or some sort of inflation measure, e.g. increases in the Consumer Prices Index (CPI) or Retail Price Index (RPI). Rent reviews are often 'upward-only', so the income stream produced provides long-term inflation protection.

- Less competition – In general, there's much less competition for commercial property than residential property. This means it's possible to achieve much higher returns, and there's much less chance of you getting gazumped.

- Potential to add value – For the creative property investor, commercial units offer great potential to add value. Not only is there the opportunity to change use classes and attract a higher rent, if you can spot an opportunity find the right tenant, there's also an opportunity to add new sources of revenue, e.g. installing ATMs and vending machines, renting out parking or storage space, allowing advertising space, or installing mobile phone towers or repeaters.

- Easier to evict tenants – If you have a tenant who stops paying their rent, then it can be easier to deal with this for a commercial than a residential property – you're not taking away someone's home and you can usually get the bailiffs in there the next day. However, although the legal aspects of evicting tenants is more straightforward, the practicalities are far from such. If your tenant is suffering due to a downturn in the wider economy, you may be evicting them at a time when it will be difficult to re-let the property to another tenant. This often means it's in your interest to work with a tenant, if they're experiencing a temporary downturn in business.

- Diversify your portfolio – Investing in commercial property gives you access to different sectors of the economy, so it can be a great way to diversify your portfolio and create an alternative income stream. You never know, it might suit your aims and objectives even better than residential property.

What are the negatives?

- Vulnerability to economic cycles – One of the downsides is that commercial property can be more vulnerable to the ups and downs of the economy. In the last global financial crises, commercial property values in the UK fell by 40% – price falls were generally much larger than for residential property.
- Valuation can be more difficult – Unlike with residential property, where it's normally straightforward to establish a value based on market comparables, valuation of commercial property is more subjective. Valuations are often based on the future cash flows a property will generate, with an adjustment for their perceived riskiness, based on the lease length and creditworthiness of the tenant.
- Due diligence needs are higher – With residential property, once the location is chosen, the amount of due diligence required is fairly light – it will typically involve just an inspection of the property, research around the likely running costs, and legal checks and searches. But with commercial property, the due diligence required is greater. You'll need to investigate the likely end tenant, typical market rents and vacancy rates for this asset, and the footfall and road traffic for the area. You'll also need to carry out an inspection of the building, covering health and safety and the internal and external condition, as well as a pest inspection. If the property is tenanted, you'll need to undertake a lease review and a review of the creditworthiness of the tenant and their business. This is no small undertaking, and many commercial investors choose work with a due diligence partner to help them with this.
- Transaction sizes are larger – It is possible to buy commercial properties at the small end of the market, for example a mixed-use property with a ground-

floor café and a flat above. But, for the most part, commercial transactions tend to be larger and require more money down, which excludes individual investors with less capital at their disposal.

- Financing is more expensive – Commercial loans tends to be more expensive, with interest rates 1% to 2% p.a. higher than typical buy-to-let mortgages on residential properties. In addition, the maximum loan-to-value is often set at 60% or 70% of the property valuation, meaning you'll need to put down a larger deposit. In most cases, the lender will insist on a repayment mortgage, rather than an interest only mortgage, which can eat into your cash flow, but this is typically offset by the higher yields.

- Voids can be much longer – Commercial units in prime locations will always attract tenants, but even so it can often take a while to find the right tenant. At the end of a lease, it's not uncommon for commercial units in high-demand areas to take up to six months to let, and you'll be responsible for the running and maintenance costs over this period. You'll need to set aside a sufficient cash buffer to cover void periods. For bespoke units in less-than-prime areas, e.g. out-of-town industrial units, it's not uncommon for these properties to take a year or more to let out, though the leases are often longer.

- Market is less liquid – There's generally a less liquid market for commercial property, meaning there are fewer transactions in the market at any one time and transactions tend to take longer. Once demand for an area has softened, it can take a long time to return, meaning that in an economic downturn you could get stuck with a property that's difficult to let out and difficult to sell. It's not uncommon for properties to sit on the market for one to two years.

- Uncertainty over the future – There's lots of uncertainty over the future and viability of UK commercial property stock. The internet is disrupting every aspect of the industry, whether it be high street retailers moving online, food delivery apps making dining-in the default, and online streaming services killing off cinemas and theatres. There's no doubt that our high streets are changing, but it's not yet clear where the chips will fall.

Valuation of commercial property

Now we've got a better idea of the pros and cons of commercial property, let's take a look at how commercial property is valued and what this means from a future capital growth perspective. Typically, commercial property is valued using the 'investment method of valuation', where we estimate the net operating profit you might expect from the property and times it by a multiple to 'capitalise' that rental profit. This valuation method is based on the formula for the capitalisation rate that I provided at the start of the book, which we can rearrange as follows:

$$Purchase\ price = \frac{Net\ operating\ profit}{Cap\ rate}$$

or

$$Purchase\ price = Net\ operating\ profit \times multiple$$

So, we can value a commercial property by taking an estimate of the net operating profit, i.e. the annual rental income from the property less the annual rental costs, excluding mortgage costs, and dividing by the desired capitalisation rate – this is equivalent to multiplying the net operating profit by a multiple, as shown.

Let's look at an example. Suppose you're interested in a commercial property in Manchester. You've done your homework, and you estimate the net operating profit is £20,000 – that is, the total of your expected rental income less your likely operating expenses is £20,000 per year. Cap rates for commercial properties do differ, depending on the property's class and location. However, for this property, the market is currently pricing off capitalisation rates of around 7% p.a. As such, our pricing multiple is worked out as (1 ÷ 0.07) = 14.3, and our expected purchase price for the property is calculated as £20,000 × 14.3 = £286,000.

You can get a feeling for suitable cap rates for properties you're interested in by checking recent sold prices for comparable properties, by speaking with local agents and valuers, or by working with a specialist property agent to support you with deal sourcing and due diligence. Capitalisation rates and valuation multiples will be influenced by the lending environment and the cost of borrowing, but they will also be influenced by the following factors:

- Property class – Different capitalisation rates and valuation multiples will be used for different classes of commercial property, depending on the risks and investor appetite for owning property in that sector.
- Location – Capitalisation rates are lower and valuation multiples higher in properties with solid locations, such as town and city centres or beachfronts, and in areas with traffic, be that foot fall or vehicle traffic.
- Tenant type – High-quality tenants, e.g. big supermarket chains or household names in other sectors, will likely be able to negotiate better terms on their rent and are seen as more secure. This will increase the valuation multiple.
- Lease length – In general, multiples will increase as the length of time left on the lease increases. Any break clauses that allow the tenant to give notice and vacate the property will reduce the valuation multiple.
- Rent reviews – A lease with an upward-only rent review linked to some kind of inflation index will likely be able to command a higher multiple, relative to an otherwise similar lease without such a provision.
- Freehold or leasehold – Owning the freehold outright can be an advantage, as it gives you full autonomy to make changes to the property and means no ground rent payments. Freehold properties generally have higher multiples.

Finally, it's worth thinking about the implications of the above for capital growth. As we've seen, with commercial property, valuations are linked to net operating profits, so commercial properties can experience capital growth when operating profits increase. Take our example above, suppose that as a result of the rent review clause in our lease, rents increase by around 3% p.a. for five years. In this case, our net operating profits might increase to around £23,000 (broadly

£20,000 × 1.15 ignoring compounding) and a valuation of the property may then increase to around £23,000 × 14.3 = £328,900 – an increase of £42,900 over five years driven solely by the rental increases baked into the terms of the lease. In practice, capitalisation rates and valuation multiples will change over time, so the actual level of capital growth experienced could be higher or lower than above. I make this point simply to illustrate that commercial properties can and do grow in value, just like residential properties, and that anything you as the owner can do to drive an increase in operating profits, be it adding an extra income stream or otherwise, can be used to drive up the value of the property.

Where to find commercial property

There are a variety of ways to go about buying commercial property in the UK, but for individual investors, the three main routes are as follows:

- Property auctions – You can find commercial properties for sale in auction rooms across the country. Commercial property lots are often mixed in with residential properties, but there are also specialist auctions dedicated solely to commercial property.
- The portals – It wasn't always the case, but portals like Rightmove and Zoopla now have dedicated sections for commercial property. These can be a great way to find opportunities, especially at the smaller end of the market. There are also a number of dedicated websites and portals for commercial property like Movehut and Propertylink. These are well worth checking out too.
- Property agents – A great way to find commercial properties is by working with a specialist agent or sourcing partner. Firms in this space will help you source investment opportunities and can support you with the due diligence needed to appropriately vet and value the property.

Keys to success

Now that we have a better feel for what commercial property is all about, let's look at some of the things you can do to increases your chances of success.

- Know your local market – Even more important than for residential property investment is knowing your target area inside out. You'll need to know what rents you can achieve for different tenant types and build up your knowledge of commercial property valuations and development costs.
- Get the right team – Important members of your commercial property team include your broker, your solicitor and your property agent. This is an area where a valuation expert can be helpful, especially if the deal or the existing lease is complex or unusual in some way.
- Carry out a lease review – There's a perception that commercial leases are more complicated than residential ones, and this can be true in some cases, particular for older leases. Modern leases are now fairly standard and much easier to read. That said, you'll still want your solicitor to do a review.
- Conduct a site inspection – You can start your due diligence with a desktop review of the opportunity, e.g. with area research and a review of the tenant and the lease, but at some point you'll need to conduct a physical inspection of the site to assess the quality of construction and the building's condition.
- It's all about the tenant – With commercial property, the tenant is even more critical to the investment's profitability. If you're buying a tenanted property, analysis of the current tenant and their business will help you determine the longevity of their business and the likelihood they'll renew their lease.
- Have a back-up plan – If you're buying a property untenanted, it's useful to have two or three plans for the site, in case the first option falls through.
- Become an expert – When you're starting out, it's best to become an expert in one class of properties and develop your knowledge out from there. Each property class has its own quirks, and understanding these differences will increase your chances of success in your chosen investment class.

- Work your way up – Also, make sure to start out small, e.g. perhaps with the purchase of a mixed-use property with commercial and residential aspects, and build up the deal size over time. As with residential purchases, those early deals are unlikely to be your best, so start out small.

Once you've sourced an opportunity and got the deal over the line, you'll likely want to employ the services of a specialist letting agent to deal with the ongoing management. This will include dealing with items like lease reviews, resolving disputes, attending to repairs, taking out appropriate insurance, and arranging any safety inspections required. It will also include marketing and advertising the property to prospective tenants at the end of an existing lease.

You should choose to work with a specialist letting agent that has a strong track record with commercial property, particularly in the class of commercial property you've acquired. They need to be able to provide all the services you're likely to require. Choosing the right agent and partner will be an important factor for success with this strategy, so don't overlook this. And unless you have a strong track record of managing commercial properties yourself, I would encourage you not to go this alone, at least until you've built up your experience and expertise in the sector over a number of years.

Further reading and useful resources

If the material in this play has piqued your interest and you want to learn more, here are three great books to take your knowledge a little bit further.

1. Palise, S. (2020). *Commercial Property Investing Explained Simply.* MSP.
2. Isaac, D., O'Leary, J. (2012). *Property Valuation Principles.* Red Globe Press.
3. Morri, G., Benedetto, P. (2019). *Commercial Property Valuation.* Wiley.

Play # 46 – Investing in a property fund

Kristi and Bryce were different to other property investors out there. Yes, they invested in buy-to-lets, but they also invested in property funds, seeing this as a hands-off way to grow a diversified property portfolio that took care of itself. Over a 15-year period, by saving hard and living frugally, they grew a £500,000 investment portfolio entirely invested in REITs and which paid them £2,500 per month. Combined with the profit from their four buy-to-lets, it was enough for them to reach financial independence.

Property without all the problems

What if I told you that there was a way to invest in property, gaining exposure to all the upsides like rental profits and capital growth, but without all the hassle? What if I told you you'd never have to take out a mortgage, spend time chasing solicitors, or deal with problem tenants? That's where our next play, investing in a property fund, comes into its own. Yes, it's an entirely different way to invest in property, and investing in a fund has both advantages and disadvantages versus direct property investment, but it wouldn't be right to go through two books on property investment without talking about property funds and how you might take advantage of them to meet your investment goals. In this play, we're going to look at what a property fund is, at the pros and cons versus direct investment, and at how to go about researching the different property funds out there.

An introduction to property funds

What is a property fund?

A property fund is a type of investment fund that invests exclusively in property. With property funds, groups of investors pool their money together, and the fund invests this money on their behalf. Each individual investor owns a small fraction of the fund and the overall property portfolio, and the day-to-day management of the portfolio is delegated to the fund. As such, individual investors do not make decisions about how a fund's assets are invested; they simply choose a fund to invest in, based on the fund's goals, fees and other factors. It's the fund manager who oversees the fund and decides what assets it should hold. In short, you put money into the fund, the fund goes out and buys property on your behalf, and you own a small fraction of everything the fund currently owns and everything it goes on to buy in the future.

What do property funds invest in?

There are lots of different types of property fund out there, and they invest across the whole spectrum of property assets, including the following:

- Commercial property – Funds investing in commercial property can invest in everything from shopping centres and office buildings to industrial estates and care homes. It can even include things like private hospitals and airports.
- Residential property – The focus of these funds is often on generating income from purpose-built, professionally managed apartment blocks. These blocks are often designed specifically for the private rental market.
- Ground rents – Though not common, there are funds out there that invest in residential and commercial ground rents. These funds can be a great way to gain indirect exposure to ground rents as an asset class.
- Land for development – Certain property funds invest directly in land, either as a speculative investment with no plans to develop it or with the intention of adding value through development planning and planning permission.

- Land with a yield – Funds that invest in hard assets like agricultural land and forestry have become popular in recent years. Often, these assets will need specialist management, so investing through via a fund is ideal.
- Property companies – Certain funds will also invest in other property-related assets, like shares in property developers, estate agents and letting agents, or construction companies. They might even buy shares in Rightmove.

So, it's possible to use property funds to gain exposure to a variety of property assets that might otherwise be unavailable to you as an individual investor. Some of the funds out there will invest in more than one of the property investment types described above, e.g. there are funds that invest in both commercial and residential property; others will restrict their investment activities to a specific type of investment, e.g. ground rents or agricultural land. It's important to take the time to research what each fund invests in and make sure you understand the fund's investment goals and objectives.

How are these funds structured?

From a legal perspective, these funds can be set up in many different ways. Some are set up under company law as limited companies, others under trust law as trusts. More important than what legal vehicle is used to set up a fund is whether the fund is set up as an open-end fund or as a closed-end fund. Let's take a closer look at what this means.

Open-end funds

With an open-end fund, anyone can put new money into the fund at any time and anyone can take money out at any time. There's no limit to how many shares (or units) the fund can offer, meaning that the shares (or unit) are unlimited. New shares (or units) can be issued as long as there's appetite for the fund. Crucially, as new money flows into the fund, the fund will be obliged to find new assets to invest in and put the new money to good use. The flip side of this, however, is that the fund has to return money to investors on demand. The fund will keep some cash on hand to handle redemptions, but if lots of investors demand their money back at the same time, the fund manager may be forced to sell or liquidate its investments in order to pay investors back.

This set-up can lead to a run on the fund (similar to a run on the bank) which can cause problems when the fund is invested in illiquid assets like property – try selling a shopping centre at short notice. What tends to happen at times of market distress is that the fund manager will halt redemptions (yes, that means you can't get your money out). This is usually done under a 'gate provision', a clause in the fund documents that allows the fund manager to limit or halt redemptions, e.g. above a certain threshold or under certain conditions. This practice of 'gating' and halting redemptions can and does give open-end funds a bad name. If you do a quick Google search, you'll likely find all kinds of stories in the press about unhappy investors who've been denied access to their money. However, as long as you understand the risks and you're comfortable with the fact you might not be able to take your money out on demand, there's nothing inherently wrong with this structure, but it is a risk that you need to understand.

Examples of open-end funds include Open-Ended Investment Companies (or OEICs) and Property Authorised Investment Funds (or PAIFs), both of which are set up under company law. Open-end funds also include unit trusts, which are set up under trust law, and can include hedge funds and exchange traded funds (ETFs). These funds do not trade on exchanges, and they are priced at the end of each day based on the portfolio's net asset value (NAV).

Closed-end funds

With a closed-end fund, the fund raises a fixed amount of capital through an initial public offering (IPO) and then lists the shares on a stock exchange. A closed-end fund is unique in that, after its IPO, the fund issues no additional shares and the fund won't redeem – that is, it won't buy back shares. Instead, the shares in the fund can only be bought or sold on the secondary market, and as supply and demand for the shares fluctuate, the fund's stock price will move up and down throughout the trading day. Like an open-end fund, a closed-end fund has a fund manager that invests the capital that the fund has raised and oversees the day-to-day running of the portfolio.

Closed-end funds differ from open-end funds in a fundamental way. A closed-end fund raises a prescribed amount of capital only once, through an IPO, when it issues a fixed number of shares. After all the shares sell, the offering is "closed" – hence the name. No new investment capital flows into the fund. Closed-end funds don't suffer the same problems with redemptions and 'runs on the fund' as open-end funds, as any investors who want to sell their holdings can do so on the open market. Because of this, they don't need to maintain large cash reserves, leaving them with more money to invest, and they're not forced to buy and sell assets at short notice, so they can make long-term decisions without worrying about liquidity. They can make use of leverage (borrowed capital) to increase returns. As a result, closed-end funds often offer higher returns or better income streams than their open-end counterparts.

One important type of closed-end property fund that's worth covering here is a Real Estate Investment Trust (or REIT). REITs are a special type of property fund that have certain tax advantages associated with them. REITs are not taxed on rental profits and capital gains from their property rental activities; however, this tax advantage comes with certain conditions. The main one is that REITs must pay out or distribute at least 90% of their tax-exempt rental profits (but not their capital gains) to shareholders each year. This means that the usual double taxation – that is, the fund paying corporation tax and the individual being taxed on distributed dividends – is largely eliminated. You can also hold REITs in a tax efficient wrapper like an Individual Savings Account (ISA) or a Self-Invested Personal Pension (SIPP), and this can make them even more tax efficient. Finally, REITs must be listed on a recognised stock exchange, which improves liquidity by allowing a secondary market to develop. On the London Stock Exchange alone, there are more than 50 REITs with a combined market capitalisation of over $70bn investing across the retail, office, residential and other speciality sectors.

The pros and cons

Investing in property funds is a different kind of investment game, and there are both advantages and disadvantages compare with direct property investment.

What are the positives?

- All the benefits – When you invest in a property fund, you get access to all the same benefits as direct property investment, including a share of the rental profits and capital growth. Some funds even use leverage to magnify returns.

- Less money down – You can invest in a property fund with as little as a few hundred pounds, so it's possible to start investing much earlier.

- It's more hands-off – The fund manager makes the decisions and oversees the management of the portfolio. So, after you've done your initial research, it really is a hands-off investment. This is great if you're time poor.

- Access to expertise – You may be an expert in buy-to-let or HMOs but know little about commercial property. Investing in a fund gives you access to the expertise of the management team, which should help lower the risk.

- Greater diversification – Because you own a slice of the whole portfolio, your investments are better diversified and less susceptible to one-off events like extended voids or large maintenance items. Rental profits and capital growth across the fund's whole portfolio should also be smoother and less volatile.

- Access to investments – Because of its size and connections, the fund is likely to have access to deals and investments that you don't. Likewise, there are certain types of investment that are difficult for the average investor to take advantage of, either because the funds required are too large or because it's not possible to do enough of these deals to achieve sufficient diversification to reduce the risk to an acceptable level. Think how much capital you'd need to buy a shopping centre. If you want access to bigger projects, investing through a fund is likely your only option.

- Tax efficiency – Certain funds, e.g. REITs, can be very tax efficient, especially if you invest through a tax wrapper like an ISA or a SIPP.

What are the negatives?

- Loss of control – For property investors who like to make all the decisions, the loss of control that comes with investing through a fund can be a negative. You also won't be able to add value using your own skills.

- An extra layer of fees – Property funds come with extra fees and management expenses that wouldn't be there with direct property investment. However, the fund may be able to compensate for this through its access to better deals and its investment expertise. Make sure you understand the fees.

- Difficulty selling – It's not always possible to sell your stake in a fund when you want to. With open-end funds, gating at times of market stress can mean your investment is frozen, and you're unable to sell. With closed-end funds, there may not always be a liquid secondary market, even if the fund is listed on an exchange. This can be a downside to investing in a property fund.

- Visibility of prices – The fact that the market price of the fund is quoted daily can actually be a negative. It can make the value of your investment appear more volatile than a direct property investment, which can make decisions more emotive. Depending on your temperament, this can be a negative.

- Less transparent – Even after you've read the fund fact sheet and dissected the company's annual report and accounts, you can still be left with questions about what the fund actually invests in and how well the assets are being managed. This lack of transparency can be a drawback. Some funds are better than others in the level information they provide to potential investors and the type of management information they provide in their annual accounts. You might even use this to filter out some of the funds – if they're not willing to provide sufficient information to help you understand their activities, then you should think twice about investing in them.

- It can be a little boring – This might not sound like a big negative, but one of the drawbacks of investing in a property fund is that it can be a little boring. Once you've completed your research and chosen funds to invest in, there's little else to do other than sit back and wait for the dividends to roll in.

How to research a property fund

If you're interested in investing in property through a property fund, you'll need to start researching the different funds on offer. Like any other investment, it's important to do thorough research and avoid investments you don't understand. Here's a checklist of some of the areas you'll want to include in your research.

1. Investment strategy – Try to understand the investment strategy of the fund, including what type of property the fund invests in, the geographical split of the portfolio, and the key assets it owns that will drive future performance.
2. Historical performance – How has the fund performed in the past, in absolute terms and against its target return or benchmark? What have total returns, rental profits, and capital growth been like historically?
3. Annual report and accounts – The annual report will contain some excellent data on the fund and its performance. You'll find details of everything from annual profit before and after tax, earnings per share, cash flow generated by the business, and details of its assets and liabilities.
4. Fees and charges – Make sure you read the fund fact sheet and prospectus to understand the fees and charges that will be applied. The lower the fees the better, as high fees will act as a drag on fund performance over time.
5. Use of leverage – Certain property funds will use leverage, but others won't. This will depend on the aims and objectives of the fund and the regulatory environment it operates in. Judicious use of leverage can amplify returns, but poor use of leverage can add to the overall riskiness of a fund.
6. Structure of fund – We've talked about open-end and closed-end funds above. Make sure you understand the structure of the fund and the legal set-up, as well as factors that might make it difficult to sell your stake when you want to, e.g. gating clauses, lack of a liquid secondary market, etc.
7. Management team – Try to understand the track record of the management team and their areas of expertise. You need to know who you're putting in charge of your money and whether they'll be a good steward.

8. Dividends / pay-out ratio – You'll want to understand the historical pay-out ratios for the fund. If you're looking for annual income, but the fund's pay-out ratios are low, then this might not be the right fund for you. REIT's, for example, have to pay out at least 90% of their rental profits each year, so they can be an excellent choice for investors looking for cash flow.

9. Alignment of interests – Has the fund entered into related-party transactions that could create conflicts of interest, e.g. has the fund entered into contracts with other businesses owned and operated by the management team? Do the management team have a stake in the fund that would ensure their interests are aligned with yours?

If you're thinking about going down this route, you should also consider investing through a tax efficient vehicle like an ISA or a SIPP. Combined with a tax efficient property fund like a REIT, this can be a powerful formula.

Seeking help from an adviser

Finally, it's also worth pointing out that this is an area where taking independent financial advice from an Independent Financial Advisor (IFA) can be beneficial. A good IFA will be able to help you structure your affairs in a tax-efficient manner and help you narrow down your choice of property funds to those that will meet your investment goals. Remember to take the time to understand and research any recommendations your IFA makes; you absolutely should not be outsourcing important financial and investment decisions to a third-party – you need to own the decision to the same extent you would if you were picking your next buy-to-let investment. You should also remember to check how your IFAs fees are structured, whether this is a fixed fee for a set scope of work, a percentage of the assets under management, or an hourly rate. Their fees should be structured in a way that aligns their interests with yours and prevents any conflicts of interest. Ultimately, you need to make sure your IFA is working for you, not selling you lemons in order to line their own pocket.

Play # 47 – Become a lender or a finance partner

Veronique had reached financial freedom years ago. Now in her late forties and with five paid-up buy-to-let properties to her name, she had a portfolio worth £600,000 that generated £2,000 per month after tax. She was looking for a strong return on £200,000 of cash savings she had in the bank, but she didn't want to manage any more properties. That's when a friend suggested she look into property-backed loans in a poacher-turned-gamekeeper twist on her usual investment style. She certainly had the knowledge for it.

Investing in property loans

Our next play, which is all about investing in property-backed loans, is a fantastic way to earn extra interest while you're saving for that next deposit or to diversify your income streams. With this play, you're essentially becoming the lender or finance partner yourself, so it's the other side of the coin to traditional property investment. As a result, it carries a different risk profile and requires a different mindset to that needed for investing in rental properties or carrying out property development projects, although lots of the knowledge you've picked up in your other property activities will be useful here too. In this play, we're going to look at some of the benefits of investing in property-backed loans, at three ways you can become a lender or a finance partner yourself, and at some of the keys to success with this type of investment activity.

The benefits and risks of property loans

Property-backed loans are a type of secured lending where the investor provides lending to a third-party and where that loan is secured against a property, usually by way of a first mortgage charge. Property loans can be an attractive investment, with the main benefits for investors being the following:

- Regular income – The loans provide the investor with regular income in the form of interest payments on the borrowed money. The returns are usually stable and predictable, with the borrowed capital being repaid at the end.
- Downside protection – The loans are secured and backed by property, which means in the event of a default, the property can be repossessed, and this can help better shield the investor's capital from significant losses.
- Portfolio diversification – Property-backed loans have a lower correlation to assets like stocks and bonds, so they can be used to increase diversification across an investment portfolio as a whole.

So, there are great reasons to invest in property loans, but there are also risks, with the main one being that the borrower could default, and the lender will be forced to repossess the property, putting their capital at risk. The lender typically looks to manage this risk in various ways, the key ones being as follows:

(1) The lender will limit the size of the loan (or LTV) to a certain percentage of the property's value, say 60% or 70%, in order to leave sufficient headroom to repossess the property and sell it without suffering a capital loss.
(2) If the project involves development activity, any development financing will be provided in instalments, with the next instalment provided only after the previous stage works have been completed and independently certified.

In this way, the lender can take reasonable steps to protect their capital and make sure there's a good chance they'll recover 100% of that capital in the event the borrower defaults or the project goes awry in some way. However, therein lies the difference between lending against property and property investment in the traditional sense. As a property investor, you own equity in the property, and if the property goes up in value, you benefit from this directly. As a property lender, you only have downside risk. That is, if the property goes up in value, you see none of this upside, but there's always a risk that the borrower will default and your capital won't be repaid in full. Being a lender is all about risk management, making sure you have sufficient protections in place, and making sure that you achieve sufficient diversification across your portfolio.

Three ways to become a lender

Now that we understand a little about the benefits and risks involved in lending as an investment strategy, let's take a look at three ways that you could become a lender yourself, if you have some spare capital to invest.

1. Partner with a mortgage provider – A number of the new mortgage providers out there, particularly those with a FinTech focus, have platforms that allow you to loan your money to other buy-to-let investors and homeowners. You can choose the investments you're interested in, based on the target interest rate, loan-to-value, and the specifics of the project. Depending on the project, you might be able to achieve interest rates of 3% to 6% p.a. It's also possible to split your capital across a number of different potential investments. The mortgage provider takes care of all the administration and the legal aspects, and you simply act as the finance provider via their platform.

2. Partner with a bridging lender – As for Option 1, there are a growing number of bridging lenders offering outside investors the option to invest in bridging loans. Again, many of these platforms allow you to pick the investments that you're interested in based on the interest rate, loan-to-value, and specifics of the project, including whether it involves development finance. With these

being bridging loans, they offer higher interest rates of anywhere between 6% and 12% p.a. depending on the LTV and whether any additional security is offered. Again, the bridging lender will typically take care of all the legals and administration, and you simply act as the finance provider.

3. Become a joint venture (JV) partner – Lastly, our third option for becoming a lender is to become the finance partner in a joint venture of some kind. We covered joint ventures in some detail in play # 26, so I won't cover them again here. However, it's worth saying that here I'm specifically talking about the situation where you structure the JV as a financing agreement, with one party being a financial backer that charges a fixed rate of interest on their capital, rather than taking a share of the profits. If you go down this route, you'll need to get the right deal structure in place, e.g. with the finance partner taking a legal charge over the property, and you'll need to put the legal framework in place yourself, with the help of a solicitor of course.

It's worth noting that with Options 1 and 2 above, many of the platforms offering these types of investment opportunities will require you to self-certify that you're a High Net Worth individual, meaning you have an income of over £100,000 or net assets (excluding your primary residence) of over £250,000. As such, you'll likely need to meet one or more of these criteria in order to get involved with this type of lending activity, so it's probably not a strategy for new investors.

Keys to success

To get this strategy right, you'll need to put time and energy in upfront to vet each opportunity. Here are some of the keys to success and some things you'll want to think carefully about, if you want to become a lender yourself.

•   Understand the project – Is this a short-term project where the borrower is looking for bridging finance or is it a long-term mortgage? Does the project involve any element of development finance? You need to look into the detail and think through the risks involved in delivering the project.

- Choose loans that match your risk tolerance – In general, loans will be riskier if they have a higher LTV, if they're longer term, and if they involve some element of development finance. You should select investments and loans you're comfortable with, given your tolerance for risk, and make sure that the interest rate is sufficient, given the riskiness of the project.

- Check out the borrower's track record – What is the borrower's track record, and do they have a good credit history? Have they delivered similar types of projects successfully in the past and do they have the right project plan and skills and expertise in place to make this venture a successful one? What's the source of the rest of the funds going into the project and is the borrower investing some of their own money into the deal? These are questions that banks would typically ask, and you should be asking them too.

- Understand your security – As well as understanding whether the project is likely to be a success, it's also important to understand how you'll get repaid if it's not. You should try to estimate the likely market value of the property, by doing your own research into sold prices in the local market, and make sure there's sufficient buffer in the LTV. Make sure you understand how the legals are structured and that you have sufficient security in place. If you're in any doubt, have a solicitor look over the paperwork.

- Be careful with development projects – Projects involving some element of development finance can be riskier propositions outright. The risk is that the borrow defaults and you're left with a half-finished development that either needs to be sold at a knocked-down price or finished off, and you may not have the skills and expertise to complete the project yourself. Make sure that the development finance is provided in instalments and that each stage of the works is completed before the next chunk of cash is provided. Also, the track record of the borrower with these projects is absolutely critical.

- Diversify your loan portfolio – Suppose you had £50,000 to invest in property loans and that you're given the choice between investing the whole £50,000 in one high-interest bridging loan yielding 12% p.a. or five £10,000 projects yielding between 6% and 9% p.a. All other things being equal, which would you choose? For me, it's all about the diversification, and I would choose the latter. Diversification is a way to reduce your risk, particular the maximum downside risk, and I would encourage all investors to think that way.

- Get a legal agreement in place – If you're partnering with a bridging lender or a mortgage provider, lending through one of their platforms for example, then they will take care of the legals, though there's no reason you can't ask for a sample loan agreement and have your solicitor look over it the first time you lend with them. If you're going down the joint venture route, then it's up to you to make sure there's a good legal agreement in place.

- Beware the property cycle – We've talked about the property cycle at length in play # 39, and it's useful to take a moment to think about the cycle from a lender's perspective. The riskiest time to be lending is at the peak of the cycle, just before a market crash. If the borrower defaults just after property prices have fallen by 25%, then your 70% LTV loan is now looking more like a 95% LTV loan, a much riskier proposition and one where your capital could be at risk. Make sure you avoid lending in an overheated property market.

As a final word of caution, you should make sure the research and standards you apply to your lending activities are just as rigorous as your property investment activities. Above all else, think through all the things that could go wrong with the project and how you would get your capital back, if those things happened. Safety of capital is what makes this an investment, rather than speculation, and although diversification can help you manage this risk, it's no substitute for a thorough and robust research process that lets you make an informed and sensible decision.

Play # 48 – Using your (SIPP) pension to invest

When long-time buy-to-let landlord and accountant Steve decided to start his own practice, he decided he also needed his own office. Although he didn't have the funds to buy an office, he did have a decent-sized pension pot, which he could use to purchase a premises. By transferring his pension pot into a self-invested personal pension or SIPP, he used his pension savings to buy a small office, which he leased back to his business. This enabled him to own the building he operated from and benefit himself in the process.

Harness the power of pensions

As a pensions actuary myself, I'm well aware that pensions don't have the sexiest reputation. In fact, most people would rather engage in a conversation about your recycling habits than talk about pensions. However, as an advocate for financial responsibility and retirement planning, I feel somewhat duty-bound to spread the word about pensions and highlight the benefits pensions have to offer. So, if you'll indulge me just a little, I'd like to spend this next play talking about how you can use pensions as a way to invest in property, either to supplement your other property investment activities or perhaps in place of them. I can't promise to make pensions any sexier, but I can promise that by the end of this play you'll have a much better idea of where to start and how to go about it, if you want to harness the power of pensions to help you meet your property goals.

Why invest through a pension?

A pension is a fund that you pay money into during your employment years and take money out of after retirement. There are lots of different types of pension, including state pensions, company pension schemes, and personal pension plans. Here, we're just going to discuss one type of personal pension that's available in the UK, known as a self-invested personal pension (or SIPP), and how you can use a SIPP to invest in property. But before we do that, let's look at why you might consider using a pension to save for your retirement.

1. Tax relief on contributions – You can get tax relief on pension contributions up to 100% of your annual earnings. Depending on the type of pension plan and whether you're a higher rate taxpayer, you may need to claim some or all of this back via your self-assessment tax return at the end of the year.

2. Tax-free investment returns – While your savings remain in the pension plan, any investment returns earned by the fund are not subject to tax.

3. Tax-free cash lump sum – When it comes time to draw your pension, up to 25% of the accumulated fund can be withdrawn as a tax-free cash lump sum. The rest can be used to provide an income, which you'll pay income tax on.

So, saving through a pension does have some big tax advantages, particularly if you expect to be in a lower income tax bracket after retirement – it means you'll pay less tax when the money is taken out than the value of the tax relief you received on your contributions. However, the one big drawback is that you can't get access to your money until retirement age. The minimum retirement age in the UK, the earliest you can take your pension, is currently 55. The government has also expressed an intention to increase this to age 57 by 2028. That means you might have to wait a while to access your pension. For some investors, this is enough to put them off pensions altogether, despite the tax advantages.

How does a SIPP work?

A self-invested personal pension (or SIPP) is a government-approved personal pension scheme available in the UK. It's a 'tax wrapper' that has all the same tax advantages we discussed above, i.e. it allows tax rebates on contributions, but it allows for a much greater choice of investments than other personal or company (occupational) pension schemes. As such, you can use a SIPP to invest in property to a greater extent than with other pension plans.

How are SIPPs structured?

From a structuring perspective, SIPPS are single-member personal pension plans that are usually set up under a master trust framework – that is, there is one legal trust and one trustee board that governs the plan. This helps keep operating costs lower, but allows the plan to retain a strong governance framework. The SIPP provider normally acts as the trustee and has certain responsibilities; some SIPP providers also appoint the member as a joint trustee, but this is less common. The provider has overall control and is in charge of the day-to-day operations. The investments are registered in the name of the trustee, and the provider decides which investments are allowable, but it's the member who makes the investment decisions. As such, a SIPP is a product for sophisticated investors who know what they're doing and want full control of their investments.

What kinds of investments are available?

As we already noted above, a SIPP has a much wider range of investment powers than other types of personal pension. In general, the SIPPs that allow members to hold specialist investments like property will have higher charges, so you will pay for this greater flexibility. SIPPs can also borrow to purchase investments, e.g. you could raise a mortgage to part-fund a property purchase through your SIPP, so it is possible to use a degree of leverage, but there are limits around how much you can borrow. The general rule of thumb here is that you can borrow up to 50% of the value of your SIPP to finance an investment in commercial property or another business. Let's run through the kinds of investments you're permitted to hold within a SIPP generally.

- Stocks and shares – You can buy stocks and shares, both UK and overseas, as long as these are listed on a recognised stock exchange.
- Government and corporate bonds – Government bonds (e.g. UK government gilts) are loans made to the government, and corporate bonds are loans made to companies. They may pay interest and a return of the borrowed monies.
- Investment funds – You can invest in a wide range of collective investments, including property funds. We covered property funds in play # 47.
- Commercial property – SIPPs can invest in all the usual types of commercial property, including retail, office and industrial buildings. This includes direct investment in commercial property, not just commercial property funds.
- Land – You can investment in agricultural land, woodland, or land that has some other commercial use, e.g. access roads, car parks, or even quarries.
- Gold bullion – Investing in gold bullion is specifically allowed for in the SIPP legislation, provided that it is 'investment grade'.
- Derivatives – You can also use a SIPP to invest in derivatives like future and options that are traded on a recognised exchange.

So, the range of potential investments is vast, but there are also some restrictions. For example, there are investments that are permitted by the primary legislation, but which were subsequently made subject to heavy tax penalties. This includes 'exotic' assets like vintage cars, wine, stamps and fine art, as well as residential property. In practice, therefore, most SIPP providers don't allow you to hold any residential property investments, including buy-to-lets, HMOs, and residential ground rents. From a property investment perspective, that means you'll mainly be able to use your SIPP to invest in direct commercial property investments, as well as taking a stake in any property funds permitted by your SIPP provider.

What fees will I pay?

Each SIPP provider will have their own fees, and the charges can be extensive, so you need to check these out carefully before you pick a potential provider. SIPPs come in a variety of shapes and sizes with vary pricing structures and fees, but I would divide them into two main camps:

1. Low-cost SIPPs – Most investors prefer these, but their investment options are limited. They give you access to anything that can be easily traded on an online platform. At the simplest end, these SIPPs are limited to investment options like unit trusts and other pooled investments. If you're looking to hold complex assets, e.g. commercial property, you'll need to look elsewhere. Fees typically include an annual fee set as a fixed fee or a percentage of your portfolio, as well as dealing fees for buying and selling stocks or funds.

2. Full SIPPs – These SIPPs offer the widest range of investment choices. They allow you to invest in commercial property, trade stocks and options on stock exchanges, invest in gold bullion, and take stakes in hedge funds. The priciest SIPPs even allow trading in risky commodities. Fees for these SIPPs typically include a set-up fee of several hundred pounds, as well as an annual fee set as a fixed fee or a percentage of your portfolio, which can run to hundreds of pounds per year. If you invest in commercial property, there will be all kinds of extra set-up costs and fees for the annual management.

When it comes time to exit from your SIPP or when you start to take your pension, there can be extra costs and charges like drawdown fees or exit-transfer fees, e.g. for transferring funds into or out of your SIPP. This is an area you'll want to try to understand upfront, before you go down the SIPP route. It's also an area where an Independent Financial Adviser (or IFA) can add a lot of value, both in helping you get this set up the right way and making sure you're running things efficiently from a tax and ongoing fees perspective.

Keys to success

Now that we have a better feel for the different types of SIPP and how they work, let's look at some of the keys to success if you use a SIPP to invest in property.

- Pick the right type of SIPP – The range of SIPPs on offer can be overwhelming, so it helps to narrow down your choices if you know what you want it for. If you simply want to invest in property funds and REITs, a low-cost SIPP will do the trick; if you want to invest directly in commercial property, you'll need a full SIPP that allows this option.

- Take advice from an IFA – If you're thinking of setting up a SIPP, make sure you take advice from an IFA to ensure you set this up in the right way. This is particularly important if you're thinking of transferring an existing pension pot into a SIPP product, as pension transfers can be complex and you need to fully understand the impacts. A good adviser will help ensure you're fully informed and will support you in your decision making.

- Work with a reputable provider – Although SIPPs are portable, you want to be working with a reputable provider from the start. Some providers will be new to the market, others will have been providing this service for years. You need to research the provider you're going to work with, understand what they're strong at and what they're not, and make sure they're a good fit for what you're trying to achieve. An IFA should be able to help here.

- Understand fees and charges – We discussed fees above, but understanding the fees and charges you'll be faced with is important. You should make sure you read and understand the provider's terms and conditions and that you're fully up-to-speed on the costs. If you don't understand how a particular fee or charge works, speak to your IFA or to the provider and get them to explain it. This is particularly the case for commercial property investment through a SIPP, where there will be fees on purchase and sale, taking out a mortgage, administration fees, and fees for ongoing management, such as VAT returns, mortgage fees, rent reviews, etc.

- Understand the governance – You'll want to understand how the decision-making works for your SIPP. For example, can you liaise with the provider directly on decisions, or will you need to do this through an IFA?
- Think about your exit strategy – You need to check that the SIPP will allow you to draw your pension in the way you want. For example, some providers allow flexible drawdown (drawing a pension in instalments) and some don't. Make sure you'll be able to access your funds in the way you want when it comes to retirement.

Finally, I want to stress again that if you're thinking about transferring an existing pension pot into your SIPP, you should take independent financial advice from an IFA. This is even more important if you're thinking about taking a transfer from a defined benefit ("DB") pension plan – that's the technical name for older types of UK pension plan that often provide pension benefits linked to your salary and years of service for a company. These DB pension benefits can be very valuable, and the decision to take a transfer can be complex. Again, a good IFA should be able to help you understand the financial impacts of taking a transfer from a DB scheme like this and what you're giving up by doing so.

Reversal

If you only have a small pension pot, then opening up a SIPP, particularly a full SIPP, is unlikely to be cost effective. With the cost of opening and running a SIPP potentially running to hundreds of pounds each year, it's not going to be worth it, if you've only got a few thousand pounds to invest. If you're in this category, a more cost effective and still somewhat tax efficient strategy might be to invest via a stocks and shares ISA, where any investment returns earned will still be exempt from tax and you won't pay tax when you withdraw funds. With an ISA, you'll still be able to invest in things like property funds and REITS; however, you won't be able to invest directly in commercial property.

Play # 49 – Buying investment property abroad

It's safe to say that by the time Chris was buying in late 2008, the Bulgarian property bubble was pretty much ready to pop. Having grown by 50% or so in real terms and close to 100% in nominal terms between 2005 and 2008, prices fell by around 35% to 40% between 2009 and 2014, taking the value of Chris's new investment with it. Looking back, it was easy to see this was a bubble – the growth didn't reflect the fundamentals of what was going on in the wider economy. However, Chris hadn't taken the time to vet this properly, he'd simply relied on marketing brochures and hype. Never a good move.

The grass is always greener

Buying investment property abroad is a dream of many investors. The allure and mystique of owning a house on the beachfront or a trendy apartment in a vibrant city district is strong. And in the years running up to the financial crisis in 2007 to 2008, fortunes were made and lost investing in overseas property. In this play, we're going to look at the pros and cons of investing overseas, we'll consider risks unique to this strategy, and we'll discuss the keys to success, if you choose to go down this path. Don't be seduced by the idea of three weeks of sun, sea and surf in the off season – investments like this need to stack up versus all other possible property investments you could make, and it can be lots of hard work running an investment like this from a distance.

The pros and cons

Overseas property investment is in many ways similar to investing in the UK. The types of property investment and general business models you could consider will be similar to plays we've looked at previously, including regular buy-to-let, holiday lets, and serviced accommodation. So, the skills needed around finding and building the investment case, financing the deal, and building the systems needed to run the business smoothly should be familiar territory. However, there are also differences. Let's look at some of the pros and cons of overseas property investment.

What are the positives?

- You can make more money – Just as the UK has a variety of local markets, the property markets in different countries each have their own unique features. Some will be better than the UK for yields, and some will have better capital growth prospects. If you invest well, you can potentially make more money than if you kept your investment activities limited to the UK.

- Geographical diversification – If you've reached a point where your portfolio is well-diversified across different towns and cities in the UK, then you might look to other countries as a way to further diversify your portfolio. That way, you'll be less dependent on the ups and downs of the UK market.

- Currency hedging – If your lifestyle means you travel around a lot and your outgoings are mostly in one or more foreign currencies, e.g. Euros, it may not be ideal that all your rental income is in pound sterling. Investing in a country where any rental profits earned are in the same currency as your outgoings can act as a currency hedge and reduce your currency risk.

- You get to stay there – The needs of the business should always come first, but one of the positives about owning property abroad is that you might get to use the property yourself at certain times of the year. You shouldn't be using it during the peak summer months, but there's no reason why you can't grab a week or two there yourself in the off-season.

What are the negatives?

- Higher upfront costs – When buying property abroad, your upfront costs will likely be higher than if you were buying in the UK. You'll incur travel and accommodation costs searching for the right property, and the cost of using local advisors and agents will likely be higher too, as you won't have the same network at your disposal.

- Extra complexity – Without a doubt, investing abroad brings an extra layer of complexity you won't have dealt with before. You'll need to learn about all the legal aspects of buying in that specific country, as well as the tax impacts of earning profits from an overseas property. None of this is easy, and you'll likely need to take advice from tax specialists, legal advisors, and accountants to structure your affairs and protect yourself from a legal standpoint. It's not one for the dabblers and dilettantes.

- It takes more work – Getting up to speed on the ins and outs of an overseas property market is no mean feat, particularly if the country you're planning to invest in doesn't speak English. Just like when you first started investing in the UK, education is the name of the game. If you don't do this properly, you'll likely get things wrong, and your property dream could easily turn into a property nightmare.

- Running costs are higher – The running costs of your investment may also be higher. As an overseas investor, you'll likely pay higher fees for things like property management services and professional advice, and your mortgage costs may also be less competitive.

- Loss of control – Any way you slice it, investing overseas is going to involve a loss of control. There's going to be a greater distance between you and your investment, and you'll need to enlist the help of third parties and agents to help you manage the property. If you've let property out remotely in the UK in the past using the services of a letting agent, you may be more comfortable with this than if you're a hands-on landlord who's used to popping round to the property and fixing things yourself on the fly.

A closer look at the risks

Although lots of investors like the idea of investing in overseas property, there are some unique risks involved, and stepping out of your comfort zone in this way can be disastrous unless you take steps to manage these risks. Let's take a closer look at some of the risks of investing abroad.

- Political stability – We take it for granted that the UK has a stable political system, but that's not the case everywhere. Buying investment property in a stable country like France or Germany is a different proposition than buying in a country like Egypt or Turkey. You need to make sure you're comfortable with the political backdrop and that your money is safe there.

- Legal risks – The UK has a robust and effective legal system, and our Land Registry, which registers property transactions, is more than 150 years old. You need to make sure the country where you're intending to buy property has an effective legal system and that the property laws provide sufficient protection for property and landowners.

- Economic conditions – The success of your investment will be influenced by what's going on in the wider economy. Is the country headed for a recession and unemployment likely to rise, putting downward pressure on rents? Or is the country going through something of an economic renaissance, with high levels of economic growth and strong wage growth? You'll want to research and understand the economic backdrop, the main industries and sectors the country relies on, where they are in their property and business cycles, and what's going on locally in the towns or cities where you're planning to invest.

- Currency stability – Earlier we talked about currency hedging, but currency risk is the flip side of the coin. If your financial obligations are largely based in pound sterling, then earning rental profits or owning an asset in a foreign currency will introduce currency risk and volatility to your portfolio. You'll want to think hard about the stability of the currency, particularly if you may need to repatriate your profits or sell your investment at short notice.

- Infrastructure risks – If your investment is a holiday let, rather than a regular buy-to-let located abroad, then you may also be exposed to changes in local infrastructure or international travel networks servicing the destination. Say your beachfront apartment is in a small town near a local airport serviced by only one major airline. In that situation, your investment is vulnerable to the airline withdrawing flights to that location. If that happened, demand could dry up overnight. Make sure there's some redundancy built in. The property should be well-connected and accessible from several airports.

- Bubble risk – If the local property market you're buying into is booming, then it might be a great opportunity, but it might also be a bubble waiting to pop. We covered the property cycle in detail in play # 39, and the advice around avoiding the winner's curse and not buying in the latter stages of the cycle are equally valid when buying overseas property. When the bubble goes pop, it's the last one to buy in that ends up getting hurt.

- Policy and tax changes – As an overseas investor buying in a foreign market, you'll be even more vulnerable to policy and tax changes that could affect the viability of your investment. For example, there was a change to the French rules in 2012 so that property income earned by non-residents was subject to social security contributions at 15.5%. In the UK, an additional surcharge for stamp duty land tax (SDLT) will be introduced on 1 April 2021 for buyers of residential property who are not UK residents. These are just examples, but you get the idea – overseas investors are political cannon fodder.

Keys to success

Now that we have a better feel for the pros and cons and risks involved, let's turn our attention to some of the keys to success. Here are my six top tips.

1. Get clear on your goals – Are you buying the property as a holiday home, as an investment, or a mix of the two? You need to get clear on your goals and on your financial expectations from the purchase. Ideally, you want to make

sure the purchase is hitting an objective that you couldn't meet any other way, such as diversification, rather than simply being an ego trip. This goal needs to be worth it to justify the larger amount of work involved.

2. Choose the right local partner – One of the best things you can do to increase your chances of success is to find a trusted local partner. Ideally, this should be someone who invests in the area themselves. The alternative would be to work with a UK agency that specialises in sourcing deals for UK investors.

3. Become an expert – Partnering up with a local is no substitute for your own lack of knowledge. If you're going to avoid making an expensive mistake, you need to educate yourself and make yourself an expert, as you did when you first invested in the UK. Don't rely on others for the local knowledge you'll need to invest successfully. You need to build this up for yourself.

4. Learn the local language – Yes, that's right – learn the local language. Us Brits aren't too great at this in general, but don't say I didn't warn you when some item in the legal fine print comes back to bite you. If you can't get to the stage where you can read legal documents with the help of Google translate, you need to tread carefully. Make sure you employ the services of a translator or that your local partner is helping you understand the salient points.

5. Make sure the numbers work – Just because you're investing abroad doesn't mean you can forget the numbers. Make sure the property works as a cash flowing investment, and don't invest for capital growth alone. Don't rely on other people's figures, such as those presented in fancy marketing brochures. Do your own research and make sure the deal stacks up and that there's sufficient cash flow and margin for safety.

6. Understand your financing options – Don't just assume that the local finance market is anything like what we have here in the UK or that you'll be able to access lending at all. You need to understand whether it's possible to obtain finance, what kind of LTV might be available, whether mortgages are interest only or repayment, and what local borrowing rates are like. Also, you'll need to make sure everything you've learned is factored into your modelling.

Reversal

When I think about buying property abroad and the fortunes that can be made and lost, the California gold rush of 1848 springs to mind. The gold rush brought hundreds of thousands of people to the region, all in search of their own small slice of the newfound wealth and opportunity. Over the seven years from 1848 to 1855, California went from being a thinly populated ex-Mexican territory to a statehood. In 1849, a state constitution was written. San Francisco grew from a small settlement of about 200 residents to a boomtown of about 36,000. Roads, churches, schools and whole new towns were built throughout California, and a few years later, California was connected to the eastern states by railroad.

But the goldfields were also a lawless place. The fields were mainly on "public land", meaning land formally owned by the United States Government, and there were no legal rules in place and no enforcement mechanisms. The benefit to early arrivals was that gold was free for the taking, but disputes were often handled personally and violently. It's estimated that gold worth tens of billions of dollars in today's terms was recovered in the gold rush, and although this led to great wealth for a few, many who participated ended up with little more than they started with – many people also lost their lives. In fact, it was the merchants who fared the best, making far more money than the miners, through entertainment, retail, shipping, lodging and transportation.

When you're thinking about buying abroad, think about whether what you're buying into is just the latest California gold rush – a risky endeavour that could make you great wealth, but which also brings exposure to new hazards and which could potentially cause you great harm. If what you're really looking for is a long holiday, then head down to the local travel agents instead. Often, it's better to stick to what you know, and that might mean you're better off investing in the UK instead and using the profits generated to get you that holiday and time off you need. The allure of owning property abroad can be strong, so before you take the plunge, make sure what you're doing makes financial sense. If you're in doubt, it's probably best to stay away.

Play # 50 – Creating value with strong design

Thomas was best known for his work on big national advertising campaigns for a famous, well-known sports brand. Working at one of the UK's leading advertising agencies, he'd gotten his start in property relatively late, but his creative skills in design and advertising gave him an edge. Thomas's strategy was all about light refurbishments, but with an emphasis on good design. He created well-furnished, practical living spaces that stood out and allowed him to command a premium on the rents he charged. When he got it right, it allowed him to achieve an ROI close to double digits.

Good design is good business

We all know bad design when we see it, be it taps where you can't work out the hot from the cold, doors where you don't know which side to push, or microwaves with controls so complicated you'd sooner eat soup from a can. However, despite the obvious commercial benefits of incorporating good design into their products and services, only the best companies are able to do this consistently and in a way that gives them a long-term advantage. Research from McKinsey has shown that companies in the top quartile of their Design Index achieved between 4% to 6% p.a. higher revenue growth and returned 5% to 6% p.a. higher total shareholder return over a six-year period from 2013 to 2018. Other similar studies conducted by the Design Institute have yielded comparable results. The conclusion is simple

– good design is good business. And it's not just companies like Apple and Nike, this design advantage is apparent across every sector researchers have looked at. But, when it comes to property and property investment, there's little material out there about how to build good design into your property business. In the next few pages, I'm going to try to reset this balance.

In our last play, we're going to look at good interior design and how you can use it to enhance the rental returns and capital growth achieved by the properties in your portfolio. No, it's not all feature walls, designer chairs and uplighting. It's about making good design choices that help you create a living space that people will want to spend time in and will pay a premium to do so, whether that be a higher rental value or higher sale price on your next property flip. Good design doesn't have to cost any more, but it does require thought, careful planning and good attention to detail. That's what our final play of Volume 2 is all about. At the end, I'll also give you some references to my favourite design and interior design books to help get your creative juices flowing, if you're interested in finding out more these ideas.

Interior design ideas to stake your life on

The material in this chapter is largely based on the book "Plain Simple Useful" by Terence Conran, one of my favourite designers. If you're interested to learn more, please check out the full book and his other writings. In the next few pages, we're going to take a walk around a typical home and run through some key principles you'll want to keep in mind for your next property project.

General principles

Getting the basics right is often half the battle. The overall layout and flow of the property must be right for the home to function. That means making sure that the configuration of the rooms makes sense and that there are enough radiators and sockets, and that they're in the right places. It also means choosing furniture and appliances that are practical, not just decorative.

- Choice of materials – If you can, choose materials with a natural look and feel and which have the potential to wear well and improve with age. Don't look at rooms on a piecemeal basis. Instead, pick out a limited palette of colours and textures and use them throughout the property to give a feeling of unity.

- Focus on the details – Choose well-designed and well-made handles, catches, taps, sockets and switches, as well as good quality doors, door frames, and windows, and it will add a feeling of quality to the property. This is even more important for items you'll touch and handle regularly.

- Don't ignore transitional spaces – Over the course of a day, tenants will move from lounge to kitchen, bedroom to bathroom, upstairs to downstairs, many times. Transitional spaces linking areas are as important as the rooms where we spend more time. Plan these routes and keep them clean and uncluttered.

Kitchens

In many ways, the kitchen is the heart of the home. Cooking is a creative pursuit, and the best kitchens are those that are simple and encourage hands-on working. You don't need to sell the family silver to create a kitchen that works and is a joy to spend time in. Simply follow this advice, and you'll be well on your way.

- Pick the layout carefully – Single-line layouts work well in open-plan spaces. L-shaped layouts are versatile and work well in both small and larger spaces; use a carousel unit in the right-angle to avoid dead space. Galley or U-shaped layouts work well when space is really tight and provide maximum storage – there should be at least 2m between the arms of the 'U' for ease of use. Island layouts require more floor area and are best left for large spaces.

- Small kitchens – If you only have a small space, opt for a fully-fitted layout to make the most of the space. Make sure you plan it carefully to come up with the optimal arrangement – there should be no wasted space. Build in pull-out or fold-down flaps to serve as extended worktops. With equipment, choose hard-working basic items, no specialist appliances. Also, choose surfaces and finishes that are light, reflective and space-enhancing.

- Lighting – Good kitchen lighting both promotes safety and can be dialled up or down to accommodate social occasions. Make sure there's enough lighting on preparation areas so tenants are not working in shadow. Uplighting works well as general background lighting, and pendant lighting hung over a table works well for eating areas – be careful with the height of this.

- Surfaces and finishes – Kitchens should be waterproof and easy to clean, so choose surfaces that are low maintenance. Countertops should, ideally, also be resistant to heat and stains, and flooring should be non-slip. Again, choose materials that will age well – no thin laminates or cheap vinyl. Splashbacks can prevent you needing to repaint walls frequently.

- Storage and kitchen displays – Store basic condiments in daily use near the food preparation area and keep spices away from heat and light. If you're planning on having a kitchen display – that is, an area where kitchen items are on display, such as open shelving or a batterie de cuisine suspended from a metal rail – make sure you only display items used regularly.

Dining rooms

Although the separate dining room is disappearing from our houses and homes, breaking bread together is still social superglue, and it's important for bonding and for the health of our long-term relationships. As such, it's worth taking the time to carve out a nice eating area in the property, even if that is located in the middle of an open-plan living area. If you don't have much room, think about how you can achieve the same thing by using your furniture and space more flexibly.

- The kitchen/dining area – If you're going to have a dining area in the kitchen, it's best to opt for an in-line or L-shaped kitchen layout. If you can, separate the cooking area from the dining area in some way, either through the layout itself or through the furniture arrangement. Big robust tables are ideal for family kitchens and double up as space for tackling homework or projects. If you're short on space, you could consider fold-down or pull-out surfaces that double up as places to eat or think about extending out into the garden.

- The living/dining area – Another option is to build a dining area into an open-plan living area in some way. If you go down this route, try to make sure the distance between the kitchen and living/dining area is as short as possible, and that the route between the two is direct and clear of obstructions. Again, make sure the dining area is separated from the living space, by placing the dining table at one end of the space or otherwise.

- Creating a focal point – Whatever the shape of the dining table, make sure there's enough room around it for people to move chairs comfortably. If you can, set up the table near a window, as a good view and natural light can give a great focal point. If you light the table with pendant lighting, make sure that it hangs at the right height – too low and you'll restrict views across the table, and you may hit your head. If you're looking for a more intimate atmosphere, you can think about dimmers or adding a few candles.

Living rooms

Gone are the days of living rooms being used just to entertain guests. These days, living rooms are vibrant, multi-purpose spaces accommodating lots of different uses, especially in family homes with children present. Above all else, they should be an area for relaxing and they should be comfortable.

- Sofas and chairs – If you're going to furnish a property, getting large furniture items like sofas correct is important. Go for simple, clean designs and classic shapes that won't date. Solid colours are good – grey and blue are recessive shades that visually minimise bulkiness. Plain upholstery can be dressed up with throws and cushions to add some colour. A grouping of different chairs can be friendly and welcoming, so think about adding in an armchair, a classic club chair, or an upright-side chair to add a sense of character.

- Lighting – Try to get as much natural light into your living room as you can, preferably from two aspects. Large mirrors hung opposite windows spread natural light around, as do filmy curtains and simple, cotton drapery. If you're short on natural light, pale flooring and light-coloured walls can help make the most of the light you do have. When it comes to artificial lighting, a bright, overhead light from a single source creates a dead atmosphere that throws off shadows and shrinks the space – instead, use multiple light sources, and try to reflect light off larger walls and ceilings.

- More about focal points – Living rooms are largely unfitted spaces, meaning the furniture defines the layout. To bring it together, you need to create some kind of focal point. This could be a colourful rug, a coffee table, or an original fireplace, if you have one. Try not to make the TV the focal point – if you can, hide the TV in a built-in cupboard or behind a sliding screen. Alternatively, put the TV on a mobile stand that can be pushed aside when not in use.

- Visual displays and collections – Adding a visual display and giving the eye something to focus on can help to generate a sense of welcome. This could be done with decorative objects like paintings and pictures, groupings of objects on a table or shelf, or with soft furnishings like throws and cushions. Enhance a collection of objects with spotlights, uplighting or backlighting.

- Storage – It's often overlooked, but living rooms have great storage potential. In multi-use living areas, especially those that double up as home offices or dining areas, good organisation and storage is key. In general, you should use wall space for shelving and think about how you can introduce furniture like cabinets, containers, lidded boxes and trunks, to hide away clutter.

Working rooms

No doubt about it, the age of home working is upon us, and with it the home office has grown in prominence. Creating a home office or a working space that's been decorated, equipped and furnished so that you want to spend time there is more important than ever, if you want to remain healthy and productive. Even areas like utility rooms, garages, and store cupboards can have some charm if they're fitted out with care and attention, making chores less tiresome.

- Shared spaces – A dedicated workspace is essential for long periods of hard work. If space is limited, slot a compact study area into a wall of storage or perhaps use a pull-out or fold-down desk to avoid sacrificing floorspace. In older homes, areas like hallways, landings and underneath stairs can make good working areas. Try to choose an area with natural light.

- Home offices and studies – Home offices and studies are essential for anyone earning a living from home. If you want to create a home office, pick a room with good natural light and which is peaceful and quiet. The humble garden shed can make the ultimate home office, and it's only a short commute away. Make sure you kit working spaces out with suitable task lighting; if the workspace will be used for long periods, pick an ergonomic desk chair.

- Utility rooms – Even spaces like utility rooms benefit from attention to detail. Don't just install appliances and move on – that's a missed opportunity. Take the time to pick materials that work, like waterproof vinyl floor tiles in areas with washing machines. Add shelving and cupboards to store any products, washing liquids, or bulk supplies. Add some racks and rails to help organise things, even on the back of the door.

Bedrooms

Above all else, bedrooms should be a place to unwind and relax, and absolutely nothing should come between your tenants and a great night's sleep. Let's look at some tips for arranging, decorating and furnishing bedrooms correctly.

- Picking the right bed – As with sofas in living rooms, if you're going to furnish a property, getting large furniture items like beds correct is important. Beds need to be the right size for the room and double beds need to be centrally placed to allow access from both sides. It's best to choose something simple and uncomplicated. Beds with legs can be space-enhancing, because the floor area is not interrupted, and adding plastic storage boxes can make good use of the space underneath. The mattress is the most important element – this is not an area to cut costs, even for a buy-to-let property, so buy a mattress of decent quality. Your tenants will thank you, and they may stay longer.

- Lighting and decoration – Light colours and light surfaces, such as pale wood flooring or neutral coloured carpeting, will make the most of the natural light the bedroom receives. Avoid bright colours and patterns that are too busy – these can be overly stimulating and make it difficult to sleep. As with living rooms, avoid relying on a single, overhead light, and try to build in multiple light sources. For small bedrooms, use uplighting directed at the ceiling to create a feeling of spaciousness. Add in light sources for reading.

- Clothes and storage – Built-in clothes-storage systems are generally more efficient and look best when they take up an entire wall and extend up to the ceiling. Allow a depth of 60 cm for hanging storage; drawers require a space of 1 metre in front. Make sure that whatever you buy is practical, i.e. doors must open easily and drawers and panels on runners must slide effortlessly. In children's rooms, sturdy portable plastic boxes are great for storing toys, and clothes can usually be stored in a simple chest of drawers.

Bathrooms

Bathing is about hygiene, but it's also about relaxation, daydreaming and letting go of stress. It can also be a creative space – I do some of my best thinking in the shower. Good bathrooms should be a joy to spend time in, but they should also be practical and easy to keep clean. Let's take a closer look.

- Space and layout – Bathrooms and shower rooms are often short on space, so good planning is essential. You need to leave at least 70 cm of space in front of toilets, showers, sinks and bathtubs, as well as 20 cm either side of the sink, in order to make the fixtures accessible and easy-to-use. Arrange the layout so the toilet is screened in some way from the bathtub or so that it doesn't align with the head of the tub.

- Family bathrooms – Where you have a decent space to work with, you should opt for a family bathroom. Allow extra room around the tub for helping out at bath-time; install twin sinks and a shower cubicle to add versatility and speed up morning preparation. All surfaces should be fully waterproof, so be generous with wall tiling and use waterproof paint.

- Showers and wet rooms – In general, I steer clear of wet rooms for buy-to-let properties, as they require careful construction and ongoing maintenance to prevent moisture seeping into surfaces and causing damage. For showers, ceramic shower trays are a great base, as they are strong and stable; cubicles with frameless doors are great for a neater, minimalist look. Choose shower controls that are easy to operate and that maintain a reliable temperature – mixers often don't. Larger tiles on the walls will prevent more leaks.

- Choosing fixtures – Avoid coloured bathroom fixtures, as they date easily. For fixtures like bathtubs, sinks and toilets, stick to classic white – it is practical and space enhancing. Tubs should be comfortable, that is, both long enough and deep enough to fit the frame of the average person. Sinks should be big enough for the intended use. Avoid small corner sinks in main bathrooms.

- Lighting – There's no legal requirement for bathrooms to have a window, but natural light is a bonus. When installing lighting, safety is key. All light fittings should be designed for bathroom use and enclosed in a waterproof casing. The type and position of switches must comply with regulations. Mirrors that are lit all the way around or to both sides give pleasing reflections.

- Surfaces and finishes – Surfaces that might be open to water and splashing, i.e. around bathtubs, showers, and sinks, need to be fully waterproof, i.e. clad in some impervious material and sealed. All other areas should be made water-resistant, e.g. using special paints. Pay attention to seals and joints. Use flooring materials that provide a little grip to prevent slipping.

Further reading and useful resources

That brings us to the end of our chapter in interior design. If the material in this chapter has sparked your enthusiasm, and if you're interested in finding out more about good design and how you can add value to your properties using interior design, here is a reading list with nine of my favourite books to get you started.

1. Norman, D. (2013). *The Design of Everyday Things.* MIT Press.
2. Norman, D. (2005). *Emotional Design.* Basic Books.
3. Norman, D. (2016). *Living with Complexity.* MIT Press.
4. Conran, T. (2014). *Plain Simple Useful: The Essence of Conran Style.* Conran.
5. Conran, T. (2015). *Conran on Colour.* Conran Octopus Ltd.
6. Conran, T. (2006). *The Ultimate House Book.* Conran.
7. Asaroglou, V., Bonarou, A. (2013). *Furniture arrangement.* CreateSpace.
8. Kondo, M. (2017). *Spark Joy.* Vermilion.
9. Henderson, E. (2016). *Styled.* Random House Inc.

Conclusion

That brings us to the end of Volume 2 of *The Property Investment Playbook*. You now have an overview of all the strategies and techniques successful investors are using to grow their property portfolios. You've built up a working knowledge of a variety of different property sourcing techniques, some of which you'll be able to use to source below market value deals. You've learned about how to use techniques like BRRR and refinancing to expand your wealth and your portfolio and how to use the property cycle and ripple effect to speed up your progress. We've also covered a range of advanced investment techniques, including ways for income-driven investors to generate cash flow. Strategies like HMOs and rent-to-rent can offer these investors a way to change their lives quickly in a way that other approaches can't, though they're not without their share of hard work and graft. We've also looked at how to turn the tables and become a lender yourself, how to invest in property in a hands-off way using property funds and SIPPs, and at some completely new areas, like investing in commercial property.

The strategies and techniques we've covered in these two volumes are at the core of what successful property investors up and down the country are doing day in, day out, but you don't need to master them all. Some of the most successful investors I know are the ones that manage to find an approach that works for them and who stick with it for the long-term, grinding out results in all weathers, be it rain or shine. As a parting word, I hope you've enjoyed reading these books and that they've helped you pick up some new ideas and approaches and find your own property niche. Thanks for reading, and I wish you the best of luck with your future property endeavours.

Get the free resources

I've prepared some free materials to accompany the book. All you need to do to access them is head over to my website. These materials include the following:

- a spreadsheet for assessing HMO property deals
- a list of all the property auction houses in the UK
- a list of all REITs listed on the London Stock Exchange
- a list of SIPPs that permit commercial property

The spreadsheets are the ones I use personally in my own property investments. It's all completely free with no sell on. Just sign up at my website at:

www.essentialproperty.net/playbook-vol-2

Printed in Great Britain
by Amazon

40749161R00118